JOHN 3:16.5

THE REST OF THE STORY

A Practical Guide into Reading the Bible and Understanding Christianity

Luke 12:49
I have come to set the earth on fire, and
how I wish it were already blazing!

Wally Gonzalez Jr.

To my mom and dad for the life journey they released
me on. Your dedication to the church led me to my
formation. My dedication of this book goes to the mantra
that always presented itself on the walls of our home:

Joshua 24:15
"As for me and my house, we will serve the LORD."

JOHN 3:16.5 REVIEWS

Thank you, Wally, for trusting and having faith in me to assist with John 3:16.5. "The rest of the story." What a fitting title. It is an honor and privilege to be trusted with such a rare and pivotal project. I think I'll just start with, wow! I was really pleased with how the book sequentially made sense. It was like an unannounced or unknown subtle shift into a new exercise or diet. The book is as you mention, like pieces of a puzzle coming together. I couldn't put the book down once I got started! For a small book, it is loaded with information, scripture, and resources. It was enlightening to learn of the "heart" of the Bible, the four Gospels, and Acts. Your simple, steady contribution with terms and interpretations moved me forward, from the beginning to the end. I really appreciated the chapters on the harms of sins, the reparation or "atonement" of sins through reconciliation, the Mass, and the tithe. I would be remiss if I avoided to mention I went to reconciliation today! This book is like a great pair of leather shoes you never want to get rid of as it's a great go-to all the time! A great refresher for generations! May God Bless you my friend, and may He bless #John3165.

Irma Garza

This writing from Wally captures a journey of a man seeking greater understanding of the Creator. Despite being exposed to all the essentials needed to eat a Christian life he was still searching for answers to fulfill a significant void in his spiritual life. It is to be noted that the search continued although it wavered and waned from time to time. Each increment of his involvement became a "stepping stone" to the next. This all came together when he heard a testimony of conversion coupled with an invitation to join the program by a very unlikely person. This invitation, endorsed by his wife who joined him, was accepted and the rewards from it are continuing to this day. He has found the fulfillment he sought and shares this with his writings. These straightforward words he writes address many others in the world who seek understanding of the Bible, its teachings, promises, and rewards. He is convinced that his life and his family are enhanced as he strives to fulfill his purpose, now known, of God's intention for him on this earth. Those who have failed to invest themselves in their journey to God because it is too much of an effort and hard to find a place to start should find help in these writings. It is refreshing to note that although many enriching experiences often wane and are forgotten as time goes on, such was not the case here. Those enhanced with a searching spirit endure and produce much fruit.

Deacon Frank Newchurch

First, thanks, Dad, for giving me the opportunity to be one of the first to read this book and give you this review. Coming from a young adult's perspective as you were looking for, this book presents major events from the bible in a very simple way. Throughout the easy read, I learned many things that I did not fully understand.

This "bible for dummies" is short, easy, and to the point. I like the way you connect with the reader throughout the book. Your sense of humor is sprinkled well while your eagerness to spread the Word of God comes out with passion. The years of hard work you have put into "John 3:16.5" gives the reader, a very nice insight into what Christianity is and better yet what it should be. Great Job! I hope everyone enjoys this read like I did!

God is good!

Elisa R. Gonzalez, Aggie '22! Gig 'em!

The book is good! Bit by bit, section to section, chunks of information just kept coming. I was able to keep track of how the bible comes together and makes sense to you. I like how you sprinkled the book with your humor. Nice touch! Your personal engagement plus added information makes it a captivating and real read. Great job!

Armando Gonzalez

ISBN 979-8-88751-450-5 (paperback)
ISBN 979-8-88751-451-2 (digital)

Christian Faith Publishing
832 Park Avenue
Meadville, PA 16335
www.christianfaithpublishing.com

Printed in the United States of America

CONTENTS

PREAMBLE

I struggled for years discerning whether to assemble a book like this or not. Who am I to preach, teach the Word of God? Who am I *not* to preach, teach the Word of God? In January 2012, after a humble Christmas and Epiphany celebration, we were sitting at the kitchen table when my sister-in-law randomly asked, "So what are your plans for 2012?" Without really having a plan I sheepishly responded, "Something I've thought about doing is writing or assembling a book on *John 3:16* [expanded], but I don't know how or where to start." The following Tuesday at work it turned out I had been signed up for a technical writing course and another seed was released.

ACKNOWLEDGMENTS

Aminta and Wally Gonzalez—Thank you, Mom and Dad, for always encouraging and supporting myself and Mimi (sister) from day one! There was never a doubt in our home. My mom and dad have been the greatest supporters of all the things I have done in my life. They never flinched to the times I would come home and tell them I'm going to Corpus Christi, or Texarkana, or Michigan, St. Louis, New Jersey (these we're all destinations that were being presented to us before the government finally settled where they could tolerate us?) Huntsville, Alabama!

Diana Adami (sister-in-law)—Thank you for pushing me off the edge of thought. Thank you, Daniel (husband), and Delfina (Diana's cousin), for answering the encounter call to Alice in 2011. If the three of you had not answered the call, I would not have journeyed to Alice voluntarily to assist. The time spent on the road, on my own, back and forth, to Alice was special. After their encounter, Diana, Daniel, and Delfina each initiated and attended several Bible studies and they have ignited others in the studies of God and Christianity. (Daniel is a songwriter. Reference the appendix for a link to his Christian and old country songs.)

Monseigneur (Msgr.) Michael Heras. In 2002 my wife and I moved to Corpus Christi Texas, and we immediately began our search for a church to attend. My wife and I were raised "cradle Catholics" attending mass every Sunday. After a couple months of shopping for the Catholic Church of choice, we finally settled into Our Lady of Perpetual Help (OLPH) Church where my wife and son, Armando, fell in love with Monseigneur's sermons. Monseigneur had the gift of delivering a unique and powerful sermon each and every week, and my wife and son were captivated.

I, on the other hand, grew up old-school Catholic needing my Sunday missal/readings and traditional hymns in hand. OLPH, like many churches, was not the wealthiest church in town, so there were no missals in the pews. What really threw me off the sermon every Sunday was the contemporary music being played *with a drum set*, etc. through mass. As a former drummer, I was totally into the music. Unfortunately that draw distracted me from the main intents of my attendance (the Word and reception of the body and blood of Christ).

After several months of *doing* what I thought was *my duty* getting the family to church, I had an epiphany or realization of my own. I had been attending church for several months, but I really wasn't getting anything from the sermons. I kept thinking to myself, "Here I am going to church every Sunday, tithing a couple bucks, but I'm not getting anything out of it." How selfish and what a joke for me to call it a *tithe*. SMH, have mercy on me, Lord. I was not even close to what the Bible teaches us about the tithe and/or talents. I would go into these two topics, but that's really for another book.

Having grown up Catholic, listening to the Word weekly, I had concluded without a doubt that there is a God. The sole thought that there is a beginning and end to everything on earth convinced me there is no other answer that makes sense.

One Sunday, as I was contemplating the family's quickest "exodus" plan (exit), a long-haired man with a ponytail made his way up to the podium. He revealed his name to us as *Tony*, and he told the congregation about an "Alpha" experience he had been through. After mass I told my wife I had been contemplating exits every Sunday for a while. Before I dared step away from the church, I told her I knew there is a God so I asked her if she and I could go through this "Alpha" that Tony spoke about. Cora, to my surprise, said yes and the next Sunday we signed up for the class and the rest is history.

Tony Oballe. Thank you, my friend, for answering God's call and grabbing my attention. I had been scouting Tony for months asking myself, "What is this guy's story?" I had never seen such a peaceful joy in such a burly or manly man (truck driver). The joy that oozed from Tony captivated my attention practically every weekend. His long ponytail always made me criticize him internally. "Who does this guy think he is? Jesus?" When he invited the congregation from the podium, I was in. I felt from the distant and extended observation that he was very wealthy when it comes to the basics in life such as love, peace, and happiness.

Cora Gonzalez. Thank you for not hesitating on my challenge to us to attend Alpha. For years, you were our rock that never gave thought to missing mass when we were home. When we were on the road, mass was optional, until we attended Alpha.

Geraldo Hernandez. Thank you Brother G for bringing Alpha that eventually transitioned to *Real Life* to OLPH. (Reference the appendix for information on Brother G's nationally traveled BOC, "The Encounters," evangelization, preaching, teaching, praising ministry.)

Thank you to my wonderful children, Armando and Elisa, and my mother-in-law that watched them as we experienced our first Alpha retreat and encounter.

Irma Garza. Thank you, amiga, business partner, for helping me grammatically edit this publication. What a blessing you have been the last four months in pushing me through the edit to complete this book.

Deacon Frank Newchurch. Thank you from the bottom of my heart, my friend, for saying yes to the read and context consideration. What a blessing it was for you to get on it quick. In a couple days you returned the manuscript to me and gave me your unique interpretations and enhancements. Thank you so much for your personal contributions helping explain *God's salvation plan* and the *Jewish influence to the mass.* As I mentioned when you suggested I add them in, those were *way* above my pay grade. Your suggested additions keenly raise us to another level of invaluable understanding. You are such a blessing to the church. Keep giving us the powerful homilies that help interpret the readings. You have a super-special gift. If anyone is in Corpus Christi, Deacon Frank assists the priest in the early morning (08:30) daily mass at Most Precious Blood Catholic Church.

Deacon Frank almost always gives the homily or interpretation of the readings. What a blessing not only to get the interpretation of the readings but to get the history and times of what was going on to each reading. God bless you, my friend. I truly believe God would say, "Well done, good and faithful servant" (Matthew 25:21).

A *huge* shout-out goes out to the many church, Tejano, and work friends (brothers and sisters) that we made through "Sweet Home Alabama." (Stand up, ya'll. It's time to salute, LOL, it's three o'clock somewhere!) Nothing but love for our Bama family!

Our last move was back home to Corpus Christi (Body of Christ), Texas! Thank you, Jesus, for this move that threw us into a whole new level of faith/Christian realization and understanding. Our journey has traversed through several Encounters, ACTS, a Curcillo, a few Fullness of Truth Conferences, the Lay Formation program; and I've actually helped with several Christ-based adult, middle school and high school programs.

INTRODUCTION

As a Christian born into the church, I never read the Bible straight out and I rarely opened it. Yes, today I know as Catholics we read the Bible every week at mass, but it was always at minimum—a week apart. The daily and weekly mass with readings presented from the Old Testament, New Testament, and other readings (psalms, prayers, and hymns) just boggled my mind. Then add the bells, smells, and aerobics that have been passed down from the beginning, and it's tough to fully understand what all is going on.

As a child, I didn't even realize we were reading the Bible continuously. Christian brothers and sisters (classmates) from other denominations would tell me we weren't reading the Bible. While I knew that wasn't true, I didn't know exactly how to explain it. Not until I got older and began to dig deeper into what I was doing, started going above and beyond the Sunday mass, I began to better understand what all is going on with the readings, how they relate to the season and each other.

The root reason for this book is to trim or simplify the Bible story while giving some tips into what the bible is, where things are and how to read it. As a lifelong poor reader/English student, I thought if a simple book had been handed to me, maybe that would have helped me learn more about Christ and his church quicker. The book is intended to be brief with simple language for the novice reader.

As a lifelong traveler, I remember seeing tons of bibles in hotels with no pictures and billions of strange words. After just a few pages or sentences, I always placed them back. By the looks of *all* the untouched bibles I opened in hotels—they were all crisp with pages melded together from the publishing house—I would bet very few people went much further than I did in cracking open the book. None of the bibles I saw had notes or bookmarkers or any sign of life, so it told me no one was reading them. While I picked up the Bible on several occasions, it was not possible to read the Bible on the short stints I was attempting. One tip I had heard was "Don't worry about the Old Testament, just start in the New Testament. That's a much easier read." Unfortunately, when you start reading the New Testament it begins with "He, who begot him, who begot her." Befuddled by this long, chronological, and laborious presentation I was *begone* pretty quick!

The Bible story, Christ, his church, in short, are just not possible to take in on a stint or alone. This attempt at a synopsis of the Bible or Christianity allows a person to quickly take in the Bible and if they like what they see, hear, feel, at that point, they can delve deeper into other references that I will share. Through this book I'll provide hints into the Bible read and I'll reference other books or recommendations for those on a deeper mission as I once trudged.

First Lesson

As Catholics, we read the Gospels (Matthew, Mark, Luke, and John) plus the rest of the Bible on a rotation year-to-year basis. Once you start reading the Bible, you realize the four Gospels are actually all about Jesus Christ and what he did while he walked the earth *incarnate* (in the flesh/*en-carne* in Spanish). Something interesting that I learned was when you read the Bible, you will realize the first three Gospels (Matthew, Mark, Luke) each have related stories; thus, these books are referred to as the "Synoptic Gospels." These books present to us many of the same stories only they're told to us from the different author's angles and interests. The fourth Gospel, John, pretty much stands on its own. Interestingly to the Gospels, cherubim (angelic figures) are described in the Bible as having four faces: a face of an ox, a lion, an eagle, and a man. The four Gospel authors are known as evangelists. They are often represented with their attributes: *the angel (man) for St. Matthew, the lion for St. Mark, the ox for*

St. Luke, and the eagle for St. John. Sometimes you'll see these icons on the podiums where the Gospels are being read from.

Reference the books of the Bible below for a quick view, study, and explanation. Notice how the Bible is split into two major sections: the Old Testament/Covenant, Before Jesus Christ (BC), followed by the New Testament/Covenant, After Jesus Christ (AC).

Books of the Bible

Old Testament

Preface	Nehemiah	Lamentations
THE PENTATEUCH	BIBLICAL NOVELLAS	Baruch
Genesis	Tobit	Ezekiel
Exodus	Judith	Daniel
Leviticus	Esther	Hosea
Numbers	1 Maccabees	Joel
Deuteronomy	2 Maccabees	Amos
HISTORICAL INTRODUCTION	WISDOM BOOKS	Obadiah
Joshua	Job	Jonah
Judges	Psalms	Micah
Ruth	Proverbs	Nahum
1 Samuel	Ecclesiastes	Habakkuk
2 Samuel	Song of Songs	Zephaniah
1 Kings	Wisdom	Haggai
2 Kings	Sirach	Zechariah
1 Chronicles	PROPHETIC BOOKS	Malachi
2 Chronicles	Isaiah	
Ezra	Jeremiah	

New Testament

THE GOSPELS	Galatians	Hebrews
Matthew	Ephesians	CATHOLIC LETTERS
Mark	Philippians	James
Luke	Colossians	1 Peter
John	1 Thessalonians	2 Peter
Acts of the Apostles	2 Thessalonians	1 John
NEW TESTAMENT LETTERS	1 Timothy	2 John
Romans	2 Timothy	3 John
1 Corinthians	Titus	Jude
2 Corinthians	Philemon	Revelation

(Source: https://bible.usccb.org/bible)

What books are in the Catholic Bible that are not in the King James Bible? *Reference the highlighted books above.* The deutero-canonical texts held as canonical for the Catholic Church and the Eastern Orthodox Church are Tobit, Baruch, Sirach, 1 Maccabees, 2 Maccabees, Wisdom. While I'm here I think it's good to define what *Catholic* means. *Catholic* is derived from the Greek adjective *katholikos*, meaning "universal." Per the *Webster Dictionary*, it refers to a member of a Catholic Church, especially Roman Catholic; a person who belongs to the universal Christian church.

I mentioned the Old Covenant and New Covenant above. What is the meaning of *covenant?* I'll explain it as I received it by Msgr. Heras through one of our Lay Formation studies. While we have heard of *contracts,* a *covenant* is an unbreakable contract that God personally *offers* to us through his blood (death) signature. Notice how I mentioned *offers.* God does not impose *his will* on us. He offers us his *free will* to accept or reject his offer. I'll expand more on this offer through the presentation of this book.

Hebrews 13:8
"Jesus Christ is the same yesterday, today, and forever."

In many bibles, you will see in the Gospels scripts in red or *italics.* These scripts are words or *direct quotes* from Jesus as captured and given to us by the four Gospel authors: Matthew, Mark, Luke, and John.

The book of Acts (after the Gospels, also written by Luke) is the follow-on of the four Gospels where the apostles begin their mission on earth. From Acts on, you roll into the New Testament.

Notice how the Gospels and Acts fall in the middle of the Bible. They bridge the Old Testament into the New Testament. The Gospel Readings (New Testament) are where Jesus comes into the world and he brings with him God's message, his words of offer for salvation.

The Old Testament is where God himself foretells the coming of his *only begotten Son*. Jesus, only begotten Son, is the fulfillment of the Old Testament prophecy.

In 1604, England's King James authorized a new translation of the Bible aimed at settling some thorny religious differences in his kingdom—and solidifying his own power. But in seeking to prove his own supremacy, King James ended up democratizing the Bible instead. (Notice how *King* James made the changes to settle differences in his "earthly" kingdom versus God's kingdom).

The Inspiration

John 3:16
"For God so loved the world that he gave his only
Son, so that everyone who believes in him might
not perish but might have eternal life."

Thus begins the *real reason* I decided to put this book together (John 3:16). Truth shared upfront: not much of what I will be presenting through this book are my words. Some interpretations will be mine, but practically everything you will read comes directly from the Bible.

As initially a novice Catholic/Christian, who eventually read the Bible, I thought why is there not an abbreviated simplified book that any novice weekend reader/youth can pick up and read in an hour or two? Imagine a world where hotels or formation groups are supplied with an abbreviated book of the Bible versus the full-fledged complex Bible. Imagine how much more could potentially take root in an hour or two reading roughly one hundred scripture quotes versus a life-long journey of opening and closing the Bible because of the complexity and dejection. As "many of his disciples who were listening" to Jesus in the introduction of his true body and blood said,

1 John 6:60
"This saying is hard; who can accept it?"

The same was my thought in trying to feebly learn or figure out Christianity on my own. This book is too hard, too heavy, too complex, too long, the excuses went on and on.

After years of having read the Bible and having attended and helped with several retreats, something that always bothered me was the stand-alone statement of John 3:16.

I remember first spotting the stand-out statement, on a bright yellow poster, of all places, at an NFL football game. That boggled my mind. It was so far out of place to me at the time. At the time, my naive mind of where Christianity belonged or where God was, was at Mass, on Sundays, from 10:00 a.m. to 11:00 a.m. Friends would let me know they believe in God (John 3:16), thus they were saved. That bothered me because if that was 100 percent accurate, then why did we need the rest of the Bible that gave us so much other information? If that was 100 percent accurate, then why are there so many derivatives or denominations of Christianity?

What I will be presenting through John 3:16.5 is my interpretation of Christianity in a nut or "the rest of the story" (as Paul Harvey would say). In short, the Bible, Christianity, life is much greater than just holding up a single verse sign or simply proclaiming you have been saved. What I discovered as a Christian man is that God is with us 24-7, not just at Mass, on Sundays, from 10:00 a.m. to 11:00 a.m. While John 3:16 truly has hooked many Christians; two verses later John 3:18 begins reeling us in with a "but."

John 3:18
Whoever believes in him will not be condemned, "but whoever
does not believe has already been condemned, because he
has not believed in the name of the only Son of God."

My prayer and primary purpose with this short compilation of scriptures is to quickly help believers and non-believers to get familiar with the Bible, God, Jesus, and the promise of *eternal life.*

Tip one: A Bible will not be necessary to read this book, but if you are truly wanting to establish a close relationship with Christ, I highly encourage you to have a bible, a dictionary and thesaurus handy to delve deeper when you have further questions or when you feel the call to dig deeper. If you would like to order a Bible, go to the appendix in the back of the book and I'll show you where you can get a Bible ordered and/or downloaded for free. If you have a Bible and if it isn't tabbed with all the books, go to a Christian bookstore and ask for the "bible tabs." Tabs will save you a *ton* of time searching for books and you'll also use your Bible much more. With the tabs, you're going to impress your friends and family turning into a Bible ninja, jumping from one location to another. If you run into a word, verse, number, name, term, color, or other that stands out or stumps you, stop and take your time to research and learn more about what that means (there is a reason your mind is telling you to stop and do some research.) Monsignor once told us that if you want to learn what all was said and meant with a verse, go to the Bible and expand your knowledge (read what came before and after the verse). Read the book introduction and more. The things that are stopping you are the things that are calling you to that closer relationship with God—his foundational truths, fruits, and discernment.

Oh, by the way, remember I just mentioned above that there are different translations and versions of the Bibles? So if English is your primary language, I do recommend the New American Bible for the easiest read and translation. Along with some free Bible recommendations, I'll provide a link to the complete list of the USCCB's Approved Bible Translations.

Dive deeper (root cause analysis) is the base teaching into all *-logy* teachings: Scientology, phycology, and sociology. All the *-logy* studies take years and hours of study. Theology is the study of God's (*theo*) logic (*logy*). If you dig deeper, you're going to discover more about what theology (God's logic) is all about.

Another *great* source for learning about all the things the Church teaches is the Catechism of the Catholic Church (*CCC*). Publicized for the Catholic Church by Pope John Paul II in 1992, it aims to summarize, in simple book form, the main beliefs of the Catholic Church. If you have a question on; idolatry, sexuality, sin (venial/mortal), father, abortion, marriage, priest, tithing, reconciliation, the Mass, Mary, the Eucharist, and others, you will find it in the *CCC* or the *Catechism*. Know this is not your grade-school catechism that we grew up with in our younger years. This is truly a new and all-inclusive book of everything you can imagine. (Reference the appendix for a link to the Catechism of the Catholic Church.)

From the introduction of the books of the Bible above, you already know all the books and roughly where they reside in the Bible. You've got this! Let's go! The more you know, the more you will grow!

From my many attempts at reading the Bible, I know if ever I had been able to get passed the introductory confusion of the Bible (New Testament), then maybe I would have been more receptive to "the rest of the story." If ever I could have fathomed the bigger picture in a couple hours versus a life-long of years, then maybe I would have had an earlier full-fledged start into the intended "faith, hope, and love" of Christ and his church.

My gratification with this short book will come when I get a person that tells me they read my book and as a result they delved deeper into the Bible, church, and God.

I pray God blesses you. I hope this is for you, but know if this is not for you, do not fret and gift it forward. There is a reason why you picked up this book, and there is also a reason why you have gotten to this point. God loves us and he waits. God loves us, and he also wants us to spread the good news.

Luke 9:23
Jesus said, *"If anyone wishes to come after me, he must deny himself and take up his cross daily and follow me."*

Fasten your seatbelt. This book starts quickly at Jesus's crucifixion. Why? To jump into the New Testament (covenant) immediately versus reading the Bible that would drag us through the Old Testament first. The New Testament or Covenant is also what Christians live today, so it makes sense to start there.

From the New Testament I'll pull in some Old Testament scripts that sling us into God's church today.

Who is God's church? We are all part of God's church.

1 Corinthians 12:20
"We are many parts, yet one body."

Even the most negative or naïve person has a calling by God. Are you ready to answer God's call or are you even aware he is calling you? Trust that God knows you.

Luke 12:7
Even the hairs of your head have all been counted. Do not be afraid. You are worth more than many sparrows.

James 2:14
What good is it, my brothers, if someone says he has faith but does not have works?

CRUCIFY HIM, CRUCIFY HIM

The Sentence of Death

Luke 23:20–21
Again, Pilate addressed them, still wishing to release Jesus, but
they continued their shouting, "Crucify him! Crucify him!"

The Crucifixion

Luke 23:33–43 When they came to the place
called the Skull, they crucified him and the criminals
there, one on his right, the other on his left. Then Jesus
said, *"Father, forgive them, they know not what they do."*
They divided his garments by casting lots. The people
stood by and watched; the rulers, meanwhile, sneered
at him and said, "He saved others, let him save himself
if he is the chosen one, the Messiah of God." Even the
soldiers jeered at him. As they approached to offer him
wine, they called out, "If you are King of the Jews, save
yourself." Above him there was an inscription that read,
"This is the King of the Jews." Now one of the criminals hanging there reviled Jesus, saying, "Are you not
the Messiah? Save yourself and us." The other, however,
rebuking him, said in reply, "Have you no fear of God,

for you are subject to the same condemnation? And indeed, we have been condemned justly, for the sentence we received corresponds to our crimes, but this man has done nothing criminal." Then he said, "Jesus, remember me when you come into your kingdom." Jesus replied to him, *"Amen, I say to you, today you will be with me in Paradise."*

John 3:16

For God so loved the world that he gave his only
Son, so that everyone who believes in him might
not perish but might have eternal life.

The Death of Jesus

Luke 23:44–49 It was now about noon and darkness came over the whole land until three in the afternoon because of an eclipse of the sun. Then the veil of the temple was torn down the middle. Jesus cried out in a loud voice, *"Father, into your hands I commend my spirit"*; and when he had said this, he breathed his last breath. (I feel at this exact moment in time, every time we read this scripture in Mass, or when we read it as we're doing now, it is appropriate to at least stop, kneel (if you feel compelled to do it), contemplate the moment and give thanks for what Jesus just completed for us (salvation, the New Covenant is official). The centurion who witnessed what had happened glorified God and said, "This man was innocent beyond doubt." When all the people who had gathered for this spectacle saw what had happened, they returned home beating their breasts; but all his acquaintances stood at a distance, including the women who had followed him from Galilee and saw these events.

The Veils

> Exodus 26:31–33 You shall make a veil woven of violet, purple, and scarlet yarn, and of fine linen twined, with cherubim embroidered on it. It is to be hung on four gold-plated columns of acacia wood, which shall have gold hooks and shall rest on four silver pedestals. Hang the veil from clasps. The ark of the covenant you shall bring inside, behind this veil which divides the holy place from the holy of holies.

What does the tearing of the veil represent? In short, when the veil was torn, God is revealing his New Covenant that no longer is hidden behind a veil. He is unveiling or transitioning from the Old Covenant to the New Covenant where His Son is given to us for our sins.

So why would a "God" even care? Because he cares for his total united body/creation. We are many parts, yet one body.

> 1 Corinthians 12:20
> "But as it is, there are many parts, yet one body."

The question still resounds or reverberates, why would *God* care?

God's Love and Christian Life

> 1 John 4:7–11 Beloved, let us love one another, because love is of God; everyone who loves is begotten by God and knows God. Whoever is without love does not know God, for God is love.
>
> In this way the love of God was revealed to us: God sent his only Son into the world so that we might have life through him. In this is love: not that we have loved God, but that he loved us and sent his Son as expiation for our sins.

1 John 4:11
Beloved, if God so loved us, we also must love one another.

1 John 4:12–16 No one has ever seen God. Yet, if we love one another, God remains in us, and his love is brought to perfection in us. This is how we know that we remain in him and he in us, that he has given us of his Spirit. Moreover, we have seen and testify that the Father sent his Son as savior of the world. Whoever acknowledges that Jesus is the Son of God, God remains in him and he in God. We have come to know and to believe in the love God has for us.

1 John 4:16
God is love, and whoever remains in love
remains in God and God in him.

1 John 4:17–19 In this is love brought to perfection among us, that we have confidence on the day of judgment because as he is, so are we in this world.
There is no fear in love, but perfect love drives out fear because fear has to do with punishment, and so one who fears is not yet perfect in love.

1 John 4:19
We love because he first loved us.

1 John 4:20–21 If anyone says, "I love God," but hates his brother, he is a liar; for whoever does not love a brother whom he has seen cannot love God whom he has not seen.
This is the commandment we have from him: whoever loves God must also love his brother.

Matthew 5:20–26
Jesus said to his disciples: *"For I tell you, unless your righteousness exceeds that of the scribes and Pharisees, you will never enter the kingdom of heaven."*

Commentary

Christ's crucifixion (his death) was the clang like a fallen pan heard around the world.

John 3:16
"For God so loved the world that he gave his only Son, so that everyone who believes in him might not perish but might have eternal life."

Through his death we heard of the tearing of the veil. The veil opens God from a prior hidden or reserved God (reserved to only the priest that would go behind the veil in the Old Testament, or the prophets in the case of the Word) to an open God that we are able to see and receive at mass weekly, thanks to the New Testament/Covenant delivery (Bible). The New Testament God (Father, Son, Holy Spirit) is all-inclusive, all-knowing, everywhere (ubiquitous, omnipresent), listening, loving, waiting, and ever teaching, adjusting, correcting.

Moses Commands Obedience

Deuteronomy 4:1, 5–9 And now, O Israel, listen to the statutes and the rules that I am teaching you, and do them, that you may live, and go in and take possession of the land that the LORD, the God of your fathers, is giving you.

You shall not add to the word that I command you, nor take from it, that you may keep the commandments of the LORD your God, that I command you. Your eyes have seen what the LORD did at Baal-peor, for the LORD your God destroyed from among you all the men who followed the Baal of Peor. But you who held fast to the LORD your God are all alive today. See, I have taught you statutes and rules, as the LORD my God commanded me, that you should do them in the land that you are entering to take possession of it. Keep them and do them, for that will be your wisdom and understanding in the sight of the peoples, who, when they hear all these statutes, will say, "Surely this great nation is a wise and understanding people." For what great nation is there that has a god so near to it as the LORD our God is to us, whenever we call upon him? And what great nation is there, that has statutes and rules so righteous as all this law that I set before you today? Only take care, and keep your soul diligently, lest you forget the things that your eyes have seen, and lest they depart from your heart all the days of your life. Make them known to your children and your children's children.

Two common repeated themes taught through the Bible are the themes of inclusiveness, "We are many parts, yet one body," and "I am the vine and you are the branches." Throughout Jesus's incarnate walk on earth, he continually spread his and his Father's greatest desire and commandment that holds everything and everyone together—love.

John 15:16–17
It was not you who chose me, but I who chose you and appointed you to go and bear fruit that will remain, so that whatever you ask the Father in my name he may give you.
This I command you: love one another.

From here on, what I will share is how God sent his only beloved Son, Jesus, on earth and from him came the ripples of Christianity. While each ripple is separate and distinct, they all are a product of our God—God, Jesus, Holy Spirit, angels, Mary, prophets, his apostles, disciples, all the way down to you. Two points we must always remember as a ripple in the tide;

1 Corinthians 12:20
"We are many parts, yet one body."

As parts, we all have a role to fulfill for God. No role is too big, nor is it too small.

John 15:5
"I am the vine; you are the branches."

From the branches come God's intended, beautiful works—his flowers. Stand strong, be strong. You are the only flower (representation) some people will receive today or in their life.

PREPARE THE WAY OF THE LORD

The Mision of John the Baptist

Luke 1:13 The angel said; "Do not be afraid, Zechariah, because your prayer has been heard. Your wife Elizabeth will bear you a son, and you shall name him John.

Luke 3:3–9 John went throughout the whole region of the Jordan, proclaiming a baptism of repentance for the forgiveness of sins, as it is written in the book of the words of the prophet Isaiah:

"A voice of one crying out in the desert:
'Prepare the way of the Lord,
make straight his paths.
Every valley shall be filled
and every mountain and hill shall be made low.
The winding roads shall be made straight,
and the rough ways made smooth,
and all flesh shall see the salvation of God.'"

He said to the crowds who came out to be baptized by him, "You brood of vipers! Who warned you to flee from the coming wrath? Produce good fruits as evidence of your repentance; and do not begin to say to yourselves, 'We have Abraham as our father,' for I tell you, God can raise up children to Abraham from these stones. Even now the ax lies at the root of the trees. Therefore, every tree that does not produce good fruit will be cut down and thrown into the fire."

Luke 1:16
He will turn many of the children of Israel to the Lord their God.

Luke 3:10–20 And the crowds asked him, "What then should we do?" He said to them in reply, "Whoever has two tunics should share with the person who has none. And whoever has food should do likewise." Even tax collectors came to be baptized and they said to him, "Teacher, what should we do?" He answered them, "Stop collecting more than what is prescribed." Soldiers also asked him, "And what is it that we should do?" He told them, "Do not practice extortion, do not falsely accuse anyone, and be satisfied with your wages."

Now the people were filled with expectation, and all were asking in their hearts whether John might be the Messiah. John answered them all, saying, "I am baptizing you with water, but one mightier than I is coming. I am not worthy to loosen the thongs of his sandals. He will baptize you with the Holy Spirit and fire. His winnowing fan is in his hand to clear his threshing floor and to gather the wheat into his barn, but the chaff he will burn with unquenchable fire." Exhorting them in many other ways, he preached good news to the people. Now Herod the tetrarch, who had been censured by him because of Herodias, his brother's wife, and because of all the evil deeds Herod had committed, added still another to these by also putting John in prison.

John Baptizes Jesus

Luke 3:22 After all the people had been baptized and Jesus also had been baptized and was praying, heaven was opened and the Holy Spirit descended upon him in bodily form like a dove. And a voice came from heaven, "You are my beloved Son; with you I am well pleased."

John 1:6–9 A man named John was sent from God. He came for testimony, to testify to the light [God/Jesus], so that all might believe through him. He was not the light, but came to testify to the light. The true light, which enlightens everyone, was coming into the world.

Luke 1:17
He will go before him in the spirit and power
of Elijah to the hearts of fathers toward children
and the disobedient to the understanding of the
righteous, to prepare a people fit for the Lord.

John 1:10–18 He was in the world [Jesus/God], and the world came to be through him, but the world did not know him. He came to what was his own, but his own people did not accept him. But to those who did accept him he gave power to become children of God, to those who believe in his name, who were born not by natural generation nor by human choice nor by a man's decision but of God. And the Word became flesh and made his dwelling among us, and we saw his glory, the glory as of the Father's only Son, full of grace and truth.

John testified to him and cried out, saying, "This was he of whom I said, 'The one who is coming after me ranks ahead of me because he existed before me.'" From his fullness we have all received, grace in place of grace, because while the law was given through Moses, grace and truth came through Jesus Christ. No one has ever seen God. The only Son, God, who is at the Father's side, has revealed him.

John the Baptist's Testimony to Himself

John 1:19–28 And this is the testimony of John. When the Jews from Jerusalem sent priests and Levites [to him] to ask him, "Who are you?" he admitted and did not deny it, but admitted, "I am not the Messiah." So, they asked him, "What are you then? Are you Elijah?" And he said, "I am not." "Are you the Prophet?" He answered, "No." So they said to him, "Who are you, so we can give an answer to those who sent us? What do you have to say for yourself?" He said: "I am 'the voice of one crying out in the desert, "Make straight the way of the Lord,"' as Isaiah the prophet said." Some Pharisees were also sent. They asked him, "Why then do you baptize if you are not the Messiah or Elijah or the Prophet?" John answered them, "I baptize with water; but there is one among you whom you do not recognize, the one who is coming after me, whose sandal strap I am not worthy to untie." This happened in Bethany across the Jordan, where John was baptizing.

John the Baptist's Testimony to Jesus

John 1:29–34 The next day he saw Jesus coming toward him and said, "Behold, the Lamb of God, who takes away the sin of the world. He is the one of whom I said, 'A man is coming after me who ranks ahead of me because he existed before me.' I did not know him, but the reason why I came baptizing with water was that he might be made known to Israel." John testified further, saying, "I saw the Spirit come down like a dove from the sky and remain upon him. I did not know him, but the one who sent me to baptize with water told me, 'On whomever you see the Spirit come down and remain, he is the one who will baptize with the Holy Spirit.' Now I have seen and testified that he is the Son of God."

What becomes of John the Baptist after he fulfilled his prophetic duty? John fades away. Actually, we read above how John was imprisoned by Herod. In Matthew 14:1–12 we hear the story how John is eventually beheaded by Herod. As John himself said in John 3:30, "He must increase, I must decrease." The same applies to us as we strive to build stronger relationships with God. He must increase, we must decrease.

John is beheaded. That's intense but suffering is a *huge part* of the Bible that many denominations avoid or do not mention. Honestly, I am pleased that I have noticed in the last few years to decade that many of the other denominations are coming to grips with the cross, communal prayers, and suffering. I found the following meditation on John's beheading in the *Catholic Daily Reflections*. I think it touches well on suffering and the cross Jesus carried for all our sins: (Reference the appendix for a link to the meditation on Fidelity in Suffering.)

Commentary

While chapter 2 is short, it's profound. From this chapter we meet John the Baptist. His mission, as mentioned in the Old Testament, was to spread the coming of our Lord. Notice how he says he didn't know who it was but he knew he was coming. In chapter 1 we heard about the Father and the Son. In chapter 2 John foretells us of Jesus coming to release the Holy Spirit. Like a fire that starts with a spark, Christianity spread through the assignments of many, that went to many, and continue to spread today through many, but

notice too how in the following reading, not everyone may be partic-
ipating according to God's will.

John 15:5–7

"I am the vine; you are the branches. Whoever remains in
me and I in him will bear much fruit, because without me
you can do nothing. Anyone who does not remain in me
will be thrown out like a branch and wither; people will
gather them and throw them into a fire and they will be
burned. If you remain in me and my words remain in you,
ask for whatever you want and it will be done for you."

Here we begin to see how God is not only independent but
dependent as well as he releases the third part of the Trinity (Father,
Son, Holy Spirit), the Holy Spirit along with humanity to spread
the good news: "We are many parts yet one body." We are informed,
"Anyone who does not remain in him will be thrown out like a branch
to wither." While some Christian views prefer to stay away from the
reality of God's words, the reality of God is that He has an unending
love and mercy for humans who were made in His image. When we
understand God's mercy, then we realize, back to John 3:16, we still
have a chance and I'll show throughout this book how God gives us
chance after chance to go home like the prodigal son (chosen son).
God has time, and he waits with open arms.

Hebrews 13:8

"Jesus Christ is the same yesterday, today, and forever."

Some Christians and non-Christians misinterpret the expectations of perfection. All Christians are human. All Christians—yes,
even your priests, pastors, the pope—are not perfect nor greater than
God. The Bible does not make any promises of perfection other than
God who is perfect.

While I'm speaking of perfection, is the pope perfect or infal-
lible? Papal infallibility means that the pope is protected from error
when he "proclaims by a definitive act a doctrine pertaining to faith

or morals" (Catechism of the Catholic Church [CCC] 891). The pope's infallibility does not mean that he is incapable of sin or error. Recently I saw the demonstration of the pope's humble obedience to God when he visited and held mass in the shrine in Mexico. As the congregation broke for reconciliations, the first person to confess was the pope himself. As humans we are all vulnerable to *temptation,* sinful thoughts and actions. One common question asked by non-Catholics is "Why do Catholics confess to priests, or where did this *sacrament of reconciliation* come from?"

John 20:19-23

On the evening of that first day of the week, when the doors were locked, where the disciples were, for fear of the Jews, Jesus came and stood in their midst and said to them, "Peace be with you." When he had said this, he showed them his hands and his side. The disciples rejoiced when they saw the Lord. [Jesus] said to them again, "Peace be with you. As the Father has sent me, so I send you." And when he had said this, he breathed on them and said to them, "Receive the Holy Spirit. Whose sins you forgive are forgiven them, and whose sins you retain are retained."

In his plan, God continually adjusts according to our imperfections or missteps. Why did God make us imperfect? While that was not God's initial plan, that is a story that unfolded in the beginning in the story of Adam, Eve, and "the fall" (Genesis 3:1–24).

Here's an adult's eye-opener as to what reconciliation really entails. I remember as a child, my reconciliation process was pretty simple—ten questions on my personal assessment of the ten commandments:

1. Did I worship the Lord my God and only him? Yes.
2. Did I say the Lord's name in vain? Sometimes, yes. *Bad answer. Confession time.*
3. Did I keep the holy Sabbath day? Pretty much yes. *Pretty much yes? Not good enough. Confess.*
4. Did I honor my father and mother? Pretty much yes.

5. Did I kill anyone? This was an easy one. Negative, Ghost Rider.
6. Did you commit adultery? Hello, I was a child. No.
7. Did I steal? No.
8. Did I bear false witness to another? No.
9. Did I covet my neighbor's wife? No.
10. Did I covet my neighbor's goods? No.

Piece of cake. Bad words and God's name in vain were pretty much my Achilles' heel all the way until I attended my first alpha.

Remember how I mentioned I was born and raised in the church? I never matured or did anything above and beyond my childish teachings. With that said, I confessed like a child until I was in my midforties. When I went to my first retreat, I vividly remember they handed us a three-page trifold, front and back, and told us to go to a quiet place and think of what we had done throughout our lives.

The whole assembly with *over a hundred retreatants* came to a stunning hush. It was as if we had all been slammed into a solid concrete wall. You could literally hear a pin drop in the hall we were in. I was blown away as to the depth of reconciliation we were being asked to consider. Needless to say, I was facing the reality of the mess I had made all my life. Some of us were so bad that they gave us a pencil and allowed us to mark all the things we needed to confess. *Free will was and still is an option for everyone today.* The people that chose not to confess that day didn't. Some actually called it a day and left. Others came to grips with their sins overnight and confessed early the following morning.

As for myself, the big crowd—the priests, nuns, lay leaders, assistants, etc.—were all my assurance that I was definitely not the first person that had to walk this intimidating *green mile*. It was after lunch as I know they had just filled us up for the day. We were told and assured we had the rest of the day to do what we felt we needed to do. We all looked around, knowing this was going to be a tough and long day. Blessed, we had about eight priests that were brought in to help with our first real *big boy* sacrament of reconciliation (John

20:19–23). Lord knows it took all of them to get us to dinner on time that night.

I remember later in the evening, after almost all of us had gone through confessions, the guys were all hanging out in front of our dorms. You could see and feel the relief from everyone that had cleared the junk from our chests/closets. I'll be honest, my trifold had like twenty to thirty checks that I had to address. This was by far one of the hardest and most stressful admittances I've ever had to do for myself.

The good news about reconciliation is once you know what sins really are and you start to confess them, they do trickle away. Eventually with time—twenty years in my case—if you take sins seriously, you will trim them down to just having to confess every once in a while. The fact about sins is we continue to stumble and fall but the great thing about reconciliation is we're given an avenue to make amends with God. I encourage everyone: Don't just make amends with God. Make amends with your brothers and sisters as the Our Father challenges us to do each and every time we pray it.

(Reference the appendix for a link to the Adult's Guide to Confession.)

GET AWAY, SATAN!

The Temptation of Jesus (Immediately after He Was Baptized by John the Baptist)

Matthew 4:1–7 Then Jesus was led by the Spirit into the desert to be tempted by the devil. He fasted for forty days and forty nights, and afterwards he was hungry. The tempter [devil] approached and said to him, "If you are the Son of God, command that these stones become loaves of bread." He said in reply,

"It is written: 'One does not live by bread alone, but by every word that comes forth from the mouth of God.'"

Then the devil took him to the holy city, and made him stand on the parapet of the temple, and said to him, "If you are the Son of God, throw yourself down. For it is written; 'He will command his angels concerning you' and 'with their hands they will support you, lest you dash your foot against a stone.'" Jesus answered him,

"Again it is written, 'You shall not put the Lord, your God, to the test.'"

Then the devil took him up to a very high mountain, and showed him all the kingdoms of the world in their magnificence, and he said to him, "All these I shall give to you, if you will prostrate yourself and worship me." At this, Jesus said to him,

"Get away, Satan! It is written: 'The Lord, your God, shall you worship and him alone shall you serve.'"

Then the devil left him and, behold, angels came and ministered to him.

Note

Throughout the Bible you will find the introductions to each book. I highly recommend reading the introductions to each book as they foretell pertinent information as they pertain to the time, situation, and relation to other books, etc.

For the script above in this chapter the introduction to Matthew states (4:1–11) that Jesus, proclaimed Son of God at his baptism, was subjected to a triple temptation. Obedience to the Father is a characteristic of true sonship, and Jesus was tempted by the devil to rebel against God, overtly in the third case, more subtly in the first two. Each refusal of Jesus is expressed in language taken from the book of Deuteronomy (8:3; 6:13, 16). The tests of Jesus resemble those of Israel (the church) during the wandering in the desert and later in Canaan, and the victory of Jesus, the true Israel and the true Son, contrasts with the failure of the ancient and disobedient "son," the old Israel. In the temptation account, Matthew is almost identical with Luke; both seem to have drawn upon the same source.

Commentary

What this chapter shows us is even Jesus was human. Once he accepted his mission, he immediately went out into the desert to discern what he was about to do. Jesus was around thirty years old when John baptized him. Notice how Jesus fasted, secluded himself, and prayed. Notice too how the devil tempted him.

Christianity is an option. Choosing good over evil is an option. God gives everyone *free will* just as he gave free will to the devil to tempt Jesus. The devil wants us on his team; thus, temptation is on his side. Temptation is the card the devil deals. The best ways to avoid trouble, anguish, and turmoil are to follow Jesus's instructions of love, attentiveness, dedication, and obedience to God.

I found a meditation on demons in the *Catholic Daily Reflections*. (Reference the appendix for a link to the meditation on Demons Are For Real.)

Our hope is in Jesus. In Luke 4:35, Jesus rebuked him and said, "Be quiet! Come out of him!" Then the demon threw the man down in front of them and came out of him.

The following chapters continue to ripple us out into Jesus's walk/teachings through life.

THE BEGINNING OF THE GALILEAN (JESUS) MINISTRY

Matthew 4:17
"From the time after his temptation, Jesus began to preach and say, 'Repent, for the kingdom of heaven is at hand.'"

The Call of the First Disciples

Matthew 4:18–22 As he was walking by the Sea of Galilee, he saw two brothers, Simon who is called Peter, and his brother Andrew, casting a net into the sea; they were fishermen. He said to them, *"Come after me, and I will make you fishers of men."* At once they left their nets and followed him. He walked along from there and saw two other brothers, James, the son of Zebedee, and his brother John. They were in a boat, with their father Zebedee, mending their nets. He called them, and immediately they left their boat and their father and followed him.

John 1:35–51 Notice how John shares a separate but similar account as Matthew above. The next day John was there again with two of his disciples, and as he watched Jesus walk by, he said, "Behold, the Lamb of God." The two disciples heard what he said and followed Jesus. Jesus turned and saw them following him and said to them, *"What are you looking for?"* They said to him, "Rabbi" [which translated means Teacher], "where are you staying?" He said to them, *"Come, and you will see."* So they went and saw where He was staying, and they stayed with Him that day. It was about four in the afternoon. Andrew, the brother of Simon Peter, was one of the two who heard John and followed Jesus. He first found his own brother Simon and told him, "We have found the Messiah" [which is translated Anointed]. Then he brought him to Jesus. Jesus looked at him and said, *"You are Simon the son of John; you will be called Cephas."* which is translated Peter, Cephas, Petros [Greek], Kephas [Aramaic]. Per Tim Staples book "Nuts and Bolts", "When Jesus gave Simon the name 'Rock' we know it was originally given in Aramaic, a sister language of Hebrew, and the language that Jesus and the Apostles spoke." [I was listening to Joel Osteen on his iHeart podcast. The talk was on "the true you." In the talk, Joel mentioned how *Simon*, meaning "sand," is renamed *Peter* or "rock." Good stuff that goes to show how deep God, the Bible, and its words are.]

The next day Jesus decided to go to Galilee, and he found Philip. And Jesus said to him, *"Follow me."* Now Philip was from Bethsaida, the town of Andrew and Peter. Philip found Nathanael and told him, "We have found the one about whom Moses wrote in the law, and also the prophets, Jesus, son of Joseph, from Nazareth." But Nathanael said to him, "Can anything good come from Nazareth?" Philip said to him, "Come and see." Jesus saw Nathanael coming toward him and said of him, *"Here is a true Israelite. There is no duplicity in him."* Nathanael said to him, "How do you know me?" Jesus answered and said to him, *"Before Philip called you, I saw you under the fig tree."* Nathanael answered him, "Rabbi, you are the Son of God; you are the King of Israel." Jesus answered and said to him, *"Do you believe because I told you that I saw you under the fig tree? You will see greater things than this."* And he said to him, *"Amen, amen, I say to you, you will see the sky opened and the angels of God ascending and descending on the Son of Man."*

Slowly but surely the Bible shares with us what Christianity is all about. In the Old Testament we read how God tried many things, like prophets and judges, to bring the people back. Finally, God, through the New Testament, gives us his Son, Jesus, in reparation for our sins. Then we learned God did this on the account of the love for his overall creation (Genesis). We also go along and begin to discover not everyone is saved if they wish not to be saved. God gives us free will to do what we want to do, yet still God is such a merciful God. He saves us even if we are not familiar with him. Who does that? Only a God who loves.

Jesus Ministering to a Great Multitude

John 4:23–25 He went around all of Galilee, teaching in their synagogues, proclaiming the gospel of the kingdom, and curing every disease and illness among the people. His fame spread to all of Syria, and they brought to him all who were sick with various diseases and racked with pain, those who were possessed, lunatics, and paralytics, and he cured them. And great crowds from Galilee, the Decapolis, Jerusalem, and Judea, and from beyond the Jordan followed him.

The Mission of the Twelve

Matthew 9:37–38 Then he said to his disciples, *"The harvest is abundant but the laborers are few; so ask the master of the harvest to send out laborers for his harvest."*

Matthew 10:1–15 Then he summoned his twelve disciples and gave them authority over unclean spirits to drive them out and to cure every disease and every illness. The names of the twelve apostles are these: first, Simon called Peter, and his brother Andrew; James, the son of Zebedee, and his brother John; Philip and Bartholomew, Thomas and Matthew the tax collector; James, the son of Alphaeus, and Thaddeus; Simon the Cananean, and Judas Iscariot who betrayed him.

The Commissioning of the Eleven

Mark 16:14–16 [But] later, as the eleven were at table [after Jesus had been crucified and Judas had already excluded himself from the twelve], he appeared to them and rebuked them for their unbelief and hardness of heart because they had not believed those who saw him after he had been raised. He said to them, *"Go into the whole world and proclaim the gospel to every creature. Whoever believes and is baptized will be saved; whoever does not believe will be condemned."*

For three years, from the age of thirty to thirty-three, Jesus walked with his disciples by his side ever teaching, preaching and recruiting.

Luke 5:1–11 While the crowd was pressing in on Jesus and listening to the word of God, he was standing by the Lake of Gennesaret. He saw two boats there alongside the lake; the fishermen had disembarked and were washing their nets. Getting into one of the boats, the one belonging to Simon, he asked him to put out a short distance from the shore. [It is appropriate here to mention Simon's boat represents Jesus and the disciples getting into the "church."] Then he sat down and taught the crowds from the boat. After he had finished speaking, he said to Simon, *"Put out into deep water and lower your nets for a catch."* Simon said in reply, "Master, we have worked hard all night and have caught nothing, but at your command I will lower the nets." When they had done this, they caught a great number of fish and their nets were tearing. They signaled to their partners in the other boat to come to help them. They came and filled both boats so that they were in danger of sinking. When Simon Peter saw this, he fell at the knees of Jesus and said, "Depart from me, Lord, for I am a sinful man." For astonishment at the catch of fish they had made seized him and all those with him, and likewise James and John, the sons of Zebedee, who were partners of Simon. Jesus said to Simon, *"Do not be afraid; from now on you will be catching men."* When they brought their boats to the shore, they left everything and followed him.

The Conditions of Discipleship

Luke 9:23–27 Then he said to all, *"If anyone wishes to come after me, he must deny himself and take up his cross daily and follow me. For whoever wishes to save his life will lose it, but whoever loses his life for my sake will save it. What profit is there for one to gain the whole world yet lose or forfeit himself? Whoever is ashamed of me and of my words, the Son of Man will be ashamed of when he comes in his glory and in the glory of the Father and of the holy angels. Truly I say to you, there are some standing here who will not taste death until they see the kingdom of God."*

When you read the Gospels, you will see in John's closing statement:

John 21:25
"There are also many other things that Jesus did, but if these were to be described individually, I do not think the whole world would contain the books that would be written."

The same lies true with this book; while there are so many other verses that I could have captured and presented to you from the Bible, the intent of this synopsis of the Bible is simply to give you a glimpse into the possibilities of Jesus in your life as your Lord and Savior.

For more details or information, my suggestion is to join a well-grounded study group in the church of your choice. The reason I point out they must be *well-grounded* is because there are so many book-smart people teaching and preaching the Bible, but they're so grounded and not *rounded* to the Word. Make sure the church/group you pick is of God—loving, believing, fearing, and understanding to the fullness of God. Continue reading *John 3:16.5* to come to a greater understanding (rounding) into God's expectations of his family. My recommendation is read Matthew 25. Matthew 25, in short, gives a comprehensive understanding into God's expectations of his family. The reason the Bible is so long and complex is because God is ubiquitous (everywhere) and unending (timeless). The reason I like Matthew 25 so much is it's well *rounded* in God's words, ever cutting and slicing in every direction we turn. If a person ever latches onto a word, it is very likely the one word or thought will cut him/her on the way back.

Hebrews 4:12
"Indeed, the Word of God is living and effective, sharper than any two-edged sword, penetrating even between soul and spirit, joints and marrow, and able to discern reflections and thoughts of the heart."

Pick up a Bible or, better yet, download the Bible onto your smartphone (see appendix). It's unbelievable what you can find through the simple search of words.

Luke 17:5–6
"And the apostles said to the Lord, 'Increase our faith.'
The Lord replied, *If you have faith the size of a mustard seed, you would say to this mulberry tree, "Be uprooted and planted in the sea," and it would obey you.*"

JESUS ESTABLISHES HIS CHURCH

Peter's Confession About Jesus

Matthew 16:13–21 When Jesus went into the region of Caesarea Philippi he asked his disciples, *"Who do people say that the Son of Man is?"* They replied, "Some say John the Baptist, others Elijah, still others Jeremiah or one of the prophets." He said to them, *"But who do you say that I am?"* Simon Peter said in reply, "You are the Messiah, the Son of the living God." Jesus said to him in reply, *"Blessed are you, Simon son of Jonah. For flesh and blood has not revealed this to you, but my heavenly Father. And so I say to you,*

> *you are Peter, and upon this rock I will*
> *build my church, and the gates of the*
> *netherworld shall not prevail against it.*

> *I will give you the keys to the kingdom of heaven.*
> *Whatever you bind on earth shall be bound in heaven;*
> *and whatever you loose on earth shall be loosed in heaven."*

Then he strictly ordered his disciples to tell no one that he was the Messiah.

I ran into this powerful meditation on Peter in the *Catholic Daily Reflections*. It gives us another great angle on the view of Peter, the church and, more importantly, "the keys of the kingdom." (Reference the appendix for a link to the meditation on the keys of the kingdom.)

The First Prediction of the Passion

From that time on, Jesus began to show his disciples that he must go to Jerusalem and suffer greatly from the elders, the chief priests, and the scribes, and be killed and on the third day be raised.

Jesus and Peter

John 21:15–19 When they had finished breakfast, Jesus said to Simon Peter, *"Simon, son of John, do you love me more than these?"* He said to him, "Yes, Lord, you know that I love you." He said to him, *"Feed my lambs."* He then said to him a second time, *"Simon, son of John, do you love me?"* He said to him, "Yes, Lord, you know that I love you." He said to him, *"Tend my sheep."* He said to him the third time, *"Simon, son of John, do you love me?"* Peter was distressed that he had said to him a third time, "Do you love me?" and he said to him, "Lord, you know everything; you know that I love you." [Jesus] said to him, *"Feed my sheep. Amen, amen, I say to you, when you were younger, you used to dress yourself and go where you wanted; but when you grow old, you will stretch out your hands, and someone else will dress you and lead you where you do not want to go."* He said this signifying by what kind of death he would glorify God. And when he had said this, he said to him, *"Follow me."*

The History and Timeline of Popes

According to Catholic tradition, Jesus founded the papacy in the first century, when he said to St. Peter,

Matthew 16:18
"You are Peter, and upon this rock I will build my church, and the gates of the netherworld shall not prevail against it."

Those words, which now circle the dome of St. Peter's Basilica in Rome, serve as the biblical mandate for the papacy. All popes are considered symbolic descendants of Peter and are thought to hold the same chair Peter held.

Today, year 2023, Catholics are led by Pope Francis. The position has transcended nearly 2,000 years (266 popes). I remember the first time I saw the continuous list of the popes. It was at that speechless moment that it hit me how important, intricate, or continuous the church history and position have been.

As with all historical studies, the popes, along with the church, have their good, bad, and ugly stories. I won't go into any details as those are all stories on their own, but what I will remind us is we must never forget what Jesus proclaimed on the establishment of his church: *"gates of the netherworld shall not prevail."* The only way to know we are not straying from God's truth is to assure always we are following God's foundational word(s). The prevailing proof is in the pudding of the church that still lives today. Jesus never said it would be perfect. He said it would prevail.

Build Your House on the Rock

Matthew 7:24–25
Build Your House on the Rock
"Everyone then who hears these words of mine and does them will be like a wise man who built his house on the rock. And the rain fell, and the floods came, and the winds blew and beat on that house, but it did not fall, because it had been founded on the rock."

The following is a list of the popes from St. Peter transcended to St. Francis (New Advent).

1. St. Peter (32–67)
2. St. Linus (67–76)
3. St. Anacletus (Cletus) (76–88)
4. St. Clement I (88–97)
5. St. Evaristus (97–105)
6. St. Alexander I (105–115)
7. St. Sixtus I (115–125); also called Xystus I
8. St. Telesphorus (125–136)
9. St. Hyginus (136–140)
10. St. Pius I (140–155)
11. St. Anicetus (155–166)
12. St. Soter (166–175)
13. St. Eleutherius (175–189)
14. St. Victor I (189–199)
15. St. Zephyrinus (199–217)
16. St. Callistus I (217–222) Callistus and the following three popes were opposed by St. Hippolytus, anti-pope (217–236)
17. St. Urban I (222–230)
18. St. Pontian (230–235)
19. St. Anterus (235–236)
20. St. Fabian (236–250)
21. St. Cornelius (251–253); opposed by Novatian, anti-pope (251)`
22. St. Lucius I (253–254)
23. St. Stephen I (254–257)
24. St. Sixtus II (257–258)
25. St. Dionysius (260–268)
26. St. Felix I (269–274)
27. St. Eutychian (275–283)
28. St. Caius (283–296); also called Gaius
29. St. Marcellinus (296–304)
30. St. Marcellus I (308–309)

31. St. Eusebius (309 or 310)
32. St. Miltiades (311–314)
33. St. Sylvester I (314–335)
34. St. Marcus (336)
35. St. Julius I (337–352)
36. Liberius (352–366); opposed by Felix II, anti-pope (355–365)
37. St. Damasus I (366–384); opposed by Ursicinus, anti-pope (366–367)
38. St. Siricius (384–399)
39. St. Anastasius I (399–401)
40. St. Innocent I (401–417)
41. St. Zosimus (417–418)
42. St. Boniface I (418–422); opposed by Eulalius, anti-pope (418–419)
43. St. Celestine I (422–432)
44. St. Sixtus III (432–440)
45. St. Leo I (the Great) (440–461)
46. St. Hilarius (461–468)
47. St. Simplicius (468–483)
48. St. Felix III (II) (483–492)
49. St. Gelasius I (492–496)
50. Anastasius II (496–498)
51. St. Symmachus (498–514); opposed by Laurentius, anti-pope (498–501)
52. St. Hormisdas (514–523)
53. St. John I (523–526)
54. St. Felix IV (III) (526–530)
55. Boniface II (530–532); opposed by Dioscorus, anti-pope (530)
56. John II (533–535)
57. St. Agapetus I (535–536); also called Agapitus I
58. St. Silverius (536–537)
59. Vigilius (537–555)
60. Pelagius I (556–561)
61. John III (561–574)

62. Benedict I (575–579)
63. Pelagius II (579–590)
64. St. Gregory I (the Great) (590–604)
65. Sabinian (604–606)
66. Boniface III (607)
67. St. Boniface IV (608–615)
68. St. Deusdedit (Adeodatus I) (615–618)
69. Boniface V (619–625)
70. Honorius I (625–638)
71. Severinus (640)
72. John IV (640–642)
73. Theodore I (642–649)
74. St. Martin I (649–655)
75. St. Eugene I (655–657)
76. St. Vitalian (657–672)
77. Adeodatus (II) (672–676)
78. Donus (676–678)
79. St. Agatho (678–681)
80. St. Leo II (682–683)
81. St. Benedict II (684–685)
82. John V (685–686)
83. Conon (686–687)
84. St. Sergius I (687–701); opposed by Theodore and Paschal, anti-popes (687)
85. John VI (701–705)
86. John VII (705–707)
87. Sisinnius (708)
88. Constantine (708–715)
89. St. Gregory II (715–731)
90. St. Gregory III (731–741)
91. St. Zachary (741–752) Stephen II followed Zachary, but because he died before being consecrated, modern lists omitted him.
92. Stephen II (III) (752–757)
93. St. Paul I (757–767)

94. Stephen III (IV) (767–772); opposed by Constantine II (767) and Philip (768), anti-popes (767)
95. Adrian I (772–795)
96. St. Leo III (795–816)
97. Stephen IV (V) (816–817)
98. St. Paschal I (817–824)
99. Eugene II (824–827)
100. Valentine (827)
101. Gregory IV (827–844)
102. Sergius II (844–847); opposed by John, anti-pope
103. St. Leo IV (847–855)
104. Benedict III (855–858); opposed by Anastasius, anti-pope (855)
105. St. Nicholas I (the Great) (858–867)
106. Adrian II (867–872)
107. John VIII (872–882)
108. Marinus I (882–884)
109. St. Adrian III (884–885)
110. Stephen V (VI) (885–891)
111. Formosus (891–896)
112. Boniface VI (896)
113. Stephen VI (VII) (896–897)
114. Romanus (897)
115. Theodore II (897)
116. John IX (898–900)
117. Benedict IV (900–903)
118. Leo V (903); opposed by Christopher, anti-pope (903–904)
119. Sergius III (904–911)
120. Anastasius III (911–913)
121. Lando (913–914)
122. John X (914–928)
123. Leo VI (928)
124. Stephen VIII (929–931)
125. John XI (931–935)
126. Leo VII (936–939)
127. Stephen IX (939–942)

128. Marinus II (942–946)
129. Agapetus II (946–955)
130. John XII (955–963)
131. Leo VIII (963–964)
132. Benedict V (964)
133. John XIII (965–972)
134. Benedict VI (973–974)
135. Benedict VII (974–983) Benedict and John XIV were opposed by Boniface VII, anti-pope (974; 984–985)
136. John XIV (983–984)
137. John XV (985–996)
138. Gregory V (996–999); opposed by John XVI, anti-pope (997–998)
139. Sylvester II (999–1003)
140. John XVII (1003)
141. John XVIII (1003–1009)
142. Sergius IV (1009–1012)
143. Benedict VIII (1012–1024); opposed by Gregory, anti-pope (1012)
144. John XIX (1024–1032)
145. Benedict IX (1032–1045) He appears on this list three separate times, because he was twice deposed and restored.
146. Sylvester III (1045); considered by some to be an anti-pope
147. Benedict IX (1045)
148. Gregory VI (1045–1046)
149. Clement II (1046–1047)
150. Benedict IX (1047–1048)
151. Damasus II (1048)
152. St. Leo IX (1049–1054)
153. Victor II (1055–1057)
154. Stephen X (1057–1058)
155. Nicholas II (1058–1061); opposed by Benedict X, anti-pope (1058)
156. Alexander II (1061–1073); opposed by Honorius II, anti-pope (1061–1072)

157. St. Gregory VII (1073–1085) Gregory and the following three popes were opposed by Guibert ("Clement III"), anti-pope (1080–1100)

158. Blessed Victor III (1086–1087)

159. Blessed Urban II (1088–1099)

160. Paschal II (1099–1118) Opposed by Theodoric (1100), Aleric (1102), and Maginulf ("Sylvester IV," 1105–1111), anti-popes (1100)

161. Gelasius II (1118–1119); opposed by Burdin ("Gregory VIII"), anti-pope (1118)

162. Callistus II (1119–1124)

163. Honorius II (1124–1130); opposed by Celestine II, anti-pope (1124)

164. Innocent II (1130–1143); opposed by Anacletus II (1130–1138) and Gregory Conti ("Victor IV") (1138), anti-popes (1138)

165. Celestine II (1143–1144)

166. Lucius II (1144–1145)

167. Blessed Eugene III (1145–1153)

168. Anastasius IV (1153–1154)

169. Adrian IV (1154–1159)

170. Alexander III (1159–1181); opposed by Octavius ("Victor IV") (1159–1164), Pascal III (1165–1168), Callistus III (1168–1177), and Innocent III (1178–1180), anti-popes

171. Lucius III (1181–1185)

172. Urban III (1185–1187)

173. Gregory VIII (1187)

174. Clement III (1187–1191)

175. Celestine III (1191–1198)

176. Innocent III (1198–1216)

177. Honorius III (1216–1227)

178. Gregory IX (1227–1241)

179. Celestine IV (1241)

180. Innocent IV (1243–1254)

181. Alexander IV (1254–1261)

182. Urban IV (1261–1264)

183. Clement IV (1265–1268)
184. Blessed Gregory X (1271–1276)
185. Blessed Innocent V (1276)
186. Adrian V (1276)
187. John XXI (1276–1277)
188. Nicholas III (1277–1280)
189. Martin IV (1281–1285)
190. Honorius IV (1285–1287)
191. Nicholas IV (1288–1292)
192. St. Celestine V (1294)
193. Boniface VIII (1294–1303)
194. Blessed Benedict XI (1303–1304)
195. Clement V (1305–1314)
196. John XXII (1316–1334); opposed by Nicholas V, anti-pope (1328–1330)
197. Benedict XII (1334–1342)
198. Clement VI (1342–1352)
199. Innocent VI (1352–1362)
200. Blessed Urban V (1362–1370)
201. Gregory XI (1370–1378)
202. Urban VI (1378–1389); opposed by Robert of Geneva ("Clement VII"), anti-pope (1378–1394)
203. Boniface IX (1389–1404); opposed by Robert of Geneva ("Clement VII") (1378–1394), Pedro de Luna ("Benedict XIII") (1394–1417), and Baldassare Cossa ("John XXIII") (1400–1415), anti-popes
204. Innocent VII (1404–1406); opposed by Pedro de Luna ("Benedict XIII") (1394–1417) and Baldassare Cossa ("John XXIII") (1400–1415), anti-popes
205. Gregory XII (1406–1415); opposed by Pedro de Luna ("Benedict XIII") (1394–1417), Baldassare Cossa ("John XXIII") (1400–1415), and Pietro Philarghi ("Alexander V") (1409–1410), anti-popes
206. Martin V (1417–1431)
207. Eugene IV (1431–1447); opposed by Amadeus of Savoy ("Felix V"), anti-pope (1439–1449)

208. Nicholas V (1447–1455)
209. Callistus III (1455–1458)
210. Pius II (1458–1464)
211. Paul II (1464–1471)
212. Sixtus IV (1471–1484)
213. Innocent VIII (1484–1492)
214. Alexander VI (1492–1503)
215. Pius III (1503)
216. Julius II (1503–1513)
217. Leo X (1513–1521)
218. Adrian VI (1522–1523)
219. Clement VII (1523–1534)
220. Paul III (1534–1549)
221. Julius III (1550–1555)
222. Marcellus II (1555)
223. Paul IV (1555–1559)
224. Pius IV (1559–1565)
225. St. Pius V (1566–1572)
226. Gregory XIII (1572–1585)
227. Sixtus V (1585–1590)
228. Urban VII (1590)
229. Gregory XIV (1590–1591)
230. Innocent IX (1591)
231. Clement VIII (1592–1605)
232. Leo XI (1605)
233. Paul V (1605–1621)
234. Gregory XV (1621–1623)
235. Urban VIII (1623–1644)
236. Innocent X (1644–1655)
237. Alexander VII (1655–1667)
238. Clement IX (1667–1669)
239. Clement X (1670–1676)
240. Blessed Innocent XI (1676–1689)
241. Alexander VIII (1689–1691)
242. Innocent XII (1691–1700)
243. Clement XI (1700–1721)

244. Innocent XIII (1721–1724)
245. Benedict XIII (1724–1730)
246. Clement XII (1730–1740)
247. Benedict XIV (1740–1758)
248. Clement XIII (1758–1769)
249. Clement XIV (1769–1774)
250. Pius VI (1775–1799)
251. Pius VII (1800–1823)
252. Leo XII (1823–1829)
253. Pius VIII (1829–1830)
254. Gregory XVI (1831–1846)
255. Blessed Pius IX (1846–1878)
256. Leo XIII (1878–1903)
257. St. Pius X (1903–1914)
258. Benedict XV (1914–1922) Biographies of Benedict XV and his successors will be added at a later date.
259. Pius XI (1922–1939)
260. Pius XII (1939–1958)
261. St. John XXIII (1958–1963)
262. Paul VI (1963–1978)
263. John Paul I (1978)
264. St. John Paul II (1978–2005)
265. Benedict XVI (2005–2013)
266. Francis (2013—)

Along with the leader (pope) Jesus appointed a host of other people (many parts, yet one body) that support or piece together the church's mission. A *huge* thanks goes out to the New Advent website for the unbelievable amount of valuable information they provide on the popes!

Luke 10:1–9 The Lord Jesus appointed seventy-two others whom he sent ahead of him in pairs to every town and place he intended to visit. He said to them, *"The harvest is abundant but the laborers are few; so ask the master of the harvest to send out laborers for his harvest. Go on your way; behold, I am sending you like lambs among wolves."* [Remember how Jesus instructed Peter; *"Feed my lambs," "Feed my sheep," "Tend my sheep."*] *Carry no money bag, no sack, no sandals; and greet no one along the way. Into whatever house you enter, first say, 'Peace to this household.' If a peaceful person lives there, your peace will rest on him; but if not, it will return to you. Stay in the same house and eat and drink what is offered to you, for the laborer deserves his payment. Do not move about from one house to another. Whatever town you enter and they welcome you, eat what is set before you, cure the sick in it and say to them, 'The kingdom of God is at hand for you.'"*

Supporting Commentary

Lord of the harvest, Saint Augustine (354–430), bishop of Hippo (North Africa), and doctor of the church sermon 101; PL36. The gospel that has just been read to us invites us to seek out what this harvest might be of which the Lord says to us, *"The harvest is great, the laborers are few, so pray the lord of the harvest to send out workers into his harvest."* So it was that, in addition to those twelve disciples whom he called apostles (those who have been sent), he sent out seventy-two others. All of them, as his own words reveal, were sent to work at a harvest that had already been prepared. What harvest is this? They were not going to reap a harvest from the Gentiles, where nothing had yet been sown, so we must think of a harvest among the Jews. It was in order to reap this harvest that the Lord of the harvest came. But to the other peoples he sent, not reapers but sowers. Among the Jews then, there was a harvest, but elsewhere, the sowing. And it was particularly while reaping among the Jews that he chose the apostles. Harvest time had come, the harvest was ripe, for the prophets had done their sowing among them.

Did not the Lord declare to his disciples, *"You say the harvest will be a long time. I tell you, look up and see the fields ripe for harvest"* (John 4:35). And again, he said, *"Others have done the work and you are sharing the fruits of their work"* (v. 38). Abraham, Isaac, Jacob, Moses, and the prophets have done the work; they worked hard to sow the seed. At his coming the Lord found the harvest to be ripe and he sent out the reapers with the scythe of the gospel.

Like the introductions to the Bible books, it is wise to listen to approved writing such as what Saint Augustine, bishop of Hippo, wrote above.

Mark 4:26–34 Jesus said to the crowds: *"This is how it is with the Kingdom of God; it is as if a man were to scatter seed on the land and would sleep and rise night and day and the seed would sprout and grow, he knows not how. Of its own accord the land yields fruit, first the blade, then the ear, then the full grain in the ear. And when the grain is ripe, he wields the sickle at once, for the harvest has come."* He said, *"To what shall we compare the kingdom of God, or what parable can we use for it? It is like a mustard seed that, when it is sown in the ground, is the smallest of all the seeds on the earth. But once it is sown, it springs up and becomes the largest of plants and puts forth large branches, so that the birds of the sky can dwell in its shade."* With many such parables he spoke the Word to them as they were able to understand it. Without parables he did not speak to them, but to his own disciples he explained everything in private.

Psalm 36:9
For with you is the fountain of life; in your light we see light.

Romans 10:8–13 Brothers and sisters: what does scripture say? "The word is near you, in your mouth and in your heart" [that is, the word of faith that we proclaim]; because, if you confess with your mouth that Jesus is Lord and believe in your heart that God raised him from the dead, you will be saved. For with the heart one believes and is justified, and with the mouth, one confesses and is saved. For the Scripture says, "Everyone who believes in him will not be put to shame." For there is no distinction between Jew and Greek; for the same Lord is Lord of all, bestowing his riches on all who call on him. For "everyone who calls on the name of the Lord will be saved."

Commentary

In this chapter we see where Jesus establishes his church. He sets an order or structure to the disordered bunch (the apostles, disciples, so on down to the lay followers of Christ). In closing we see how the Word spreads not only from the apostles but down to the disciples, and the most crucial piece of the puzzle is ourselves. As the chapter closes, we see how Paul shared with the congregation, "The word is near you, in your mouth and in your heart." It is our duty as we meet God to share or witness forward what we see and have come to believe. As many pastors and evangelists have said, you may be the only bible the next person ever hears. It is our duty, however educated or uneducated we are, to share the story and love of Christ. Herein is where my reason comes to full fruition of putting this book together and not be concerned of what expert theologians will say.

RABBI, TEACHER/ABBA, FATHER
Jesus performs miracles, teaches, heals, and passes it forward.

The Wedding at Cana

John 2:1–11 On the third day there was a wedding at Cana in Galilee, and the mother of Jesus was there. Jesus also was invited to the wedding with his disciples. When the wine ran out, the mother of Jesus said to him, "They have no wine." And Jesus said to her, *"Woman, what does this have to do with me? My hour has not yet come."* His mother said to the servants, "Do whatever he tells you." Now there were six stone water jars there for the Jewish rites of purification, each holding twenty or thirty gallons. Jesus said to the servants, *"Fill the jars with water."* And they filled them up to the brim. And he said to them, *"Now draw some out and take it to the master of the feast."* So they took it. When the master of the feast tasted the water now become wine, and did not know where it came from [though the servants who had drawn the water knew], the master of the feast called the bridegroom and said to him, "Everyone serves the good wine first, and when people have drunk freely, then the poor wine. But you have kept the good wine until now." This, the first of his signs, Jesus did at Cana in Galilee, and manifested his glory. And his disciples believed in him.

The Lord's Prayer

Luke 11:1–4 He was praying in a certain place, and when he had finished, one of his disciples said to him, "Lord, teach us to pray just as John taught his disciples." He said to them, *"When you pray, say: Father, hallowed be your name, your kingdom come. Give us each day our daily bread and forgive us our sins for we ourselves forgive everyone in debt to us, and do not subject us to the final test."*

The Official's Daughter and the Woman With a Hemorrhage

Matthew 9:18–26 While he was saying these things to them, an official came forward, knelt down before him, and said, "My daughter has just died. But come, lay your hand on her, and she will live." Jesus rose and followed him, and so did his disciples. A woman suffering hemorrhages for twelve years came up behind him and touched the tassel on his cloak. She said to herself, "If only I can touch his cloak, I shall be cured." Jesus turned around and saw her, and said, *"Courage, daughter! Your faith has saved you."* And from that hour the woman was cured. When Jesus arrived at the official's house and saw the flute players and the crowd who were making a commotion, he said, *"Go away! The girl is not dead but sleeping."* And they ridiculed him. When the crowd was put out, he came and took her by the hand, and the little girl arose. And news of this spread throughout all that land.

The Promise of the Spirit

Acts 1:1–5 In the first book, Theophilus, I [Luke] dealt with all that Jesus did and taught until the day he was taken up, after giving instructions through the Holy Spirit to the apostles whom he had chosen. He presented himself alive to them by many proofs after he had suffered [passed away], appearing to them during forty days and speaking about the kingdom of God. While meeting with them, he enjoined them not to depart from Jerusalem, but to wait for *"the promise of the Father about which you have heard me speak; for John baptized with water, but in a few days you will be baptized with the Holy Spirit."*

Bible Introduction to Corinthians, Paul Reminds the Church of Jesus's Teachings

Paul established a Christian community in Corinth around the year 51. Paul's first letter to the church of Corinth provides us with an insight into the life of the first-generation early Christian community. Paul responds to questions addressed to him and to several situations of which he had been informed. Interesting about Paul's letter to the Corinthians is the strife, confusion, and quest for guidance into the church. Several passages of utmost importance to the church are the importance into the understanding of early Christian teaching on the Eucharist (1 Corinthians 10:14–22, 11:17–34) and on the resurrection of the body (1 Corinthians 15:1–58).

1 Corinthians 10:1–13 I do not want you to be unaware, brothers, that our ancestors were all under the cloud and all passed through the sea, and all of them were baptized into Moses in the cloud and in the sea. All ate the same spiritual food, and all drank the same spiritual drink, for they drank from a spiritual rock that followed them, and the rock was the Christ. Yet God

was not pleased with most of them, for they were struck down in the desert. These things happened as examples for us, so that we might not desire evil things, as they did. And do not become idolaters, as some of them did, as it is written, "The people sat down to eat and drink, and rose up to revel." Let us not indulge in immorality as some of them did, and twenty-three-thousand fell within a single day. Let us not test Christ as some of them did, and suffered death by serpents. Do not grumble as some of them did, and suffered death by the destroyer. These things happened to them as an example, and they have been written down as a warning to us, upon whom the end of the ages has come. Therefore, whoever thinks he is standing secure should take care not to fall. No trial has come to you but what is human. God is faithful and will not let you be tried beyond your strength; but with the trial he will also provide a way out, so that you may be able to bear it.

1 Corinthians 11:1–2
Be imitators of me, as I am of Christ. I praise you because you remember me in everything and hold fast to the 'traditions', just as I handed them on to you.

Commentary

In this chapter we start to experience God (Jesus Christ) in the flesh performing miracles both to the touch and from afar. In this chapter again we hear about the Holy Spirit that comes to spread, not to contain the Word and workings of God. Many other stories can be found in the Gospel readings that tell us of God's miracles, mercies, and love.

The first gospel reading in this chapter begins with God's first miracle. Notice how Jesus initially resists the calling: *"Woman, what does this have to do with me? My hour has not yet come."* His mother (Mary), knowing and accepting who Jesus was and what he could do (Luke 1:26–38, announcement of the birth of Jesus, "May it be done to me according to your word") simply instructs the servants, "Do whatever he tells you." Jesus, in obedience to his mother's words, accepts the fact that his time has in fact come, blesses the wedding couple in Cana. The rest is history and Jesus's mission on earth fully begins to unfold.

LAST SUPPER

Luke 22:19
"This is my body, this is my blood, do this in memory of me."

In the beginning, when God created the heavens and the earth.

The Testing of Abraham (Old Testament)

Genesis 22:1–18 Sometime afterward, God put Abraham to the test and said to him: *Abraham!* "Here I am!" he replied. Then God said: "*Take your son Isaac, your only one, whom you love, and go to the land of Moriah. There offer him up as a burnt offering on one of the heights that I will point out to you.*" Early the next morning Abraham saddled his donkey, took with him two of his servants and his son Isaac, and after cutting the wood for the burnt offering, set out for the place of which God had told him.

On the third day Abraham caught sight of the place from a distance. Abraham said to his servants: "Stay here with the donkey, while the boy and I go on over there. We will worship and then come back to you." So Abraham took the wood for the burnt offering and laid it on his son Isaac, while he himself carried the fire and the knife.

As the two walked on together, Isaac spoke to his father Abraham. "Father!" he said. "Here I am," he replied. Isaac continued, "Here are the fire and the wood, but where is the sheep for the burnt offering?" "My son," Abraham answered, "God will provide the sheep for the burnt offering." Then the two walked on together.

When they came to the place of which God had told him, Abraham built an altar there and arranged the wood on it. Next he bound his son Isaac, and put him on top of the wood on the altar. Then Abraham reached out and took the knife to slaughter his son. But the angel of the LORD called to him from heaven, "Abraham, Abraham!" "Here I am," he answered. "Do not lay your hand on the boy," said the angel. "Do not do the least thing to him. For now I know that you fear God, since you did not withhold from me your son, your only one." Abraham looked up and saw a single ram caught by its horns in the thicket. So Abraham went and took the ram and offered it up as a burnt offering in place of his son.

Abraham named that place Yahweh-yireh; hence people today say, "On the mountain the LORD will provide."

A second time the angel of the LORD called to Abraham from heaven and said: "I swear by my very self—oracle of the LORD—that because you acted as you did in not withholding from me your son, your only one, I will bless you and make your descendants as countless as the stars of the sky and the sands of the seashore; your descendants will take possession of the gates of their enemies, and in your descendants all the nations of the earth will find blessing, because you obeyed my command."

Laws of Communion Sacrifices (Old Testament)

Leviticus 3:1–17 If a person's offering is a communion sacrifice, if it is brought from the herd, be it a male or a female animal, it must be presented without blemish before the LORD. The one offering it shall lay a hand on the head of the offering. It shall then be slaughtered at the entrance of the tent of meeting. Aaron's sons, the priests, shall splash its blood on all the sides of the altar. From the communion sacrifice the individual shall offer as an oblation to the LORD the fat that covers the inner organs, and all the fat that adheres to them, as well as the two kidneys, with the fat on them near the loins, and the lobe of the liver, which is removed with the kidneys. Aaron's sons shall burn this on the altar with the burnt offering that is on the wood and the embers, as a sweet-smelling oblation to the LORD. If the communion sacrifice one offers to the LORD is from the flock, be it a male or a female animal, it must be presented without blemish. If one presents a lamb as an offering, that person shall bring it before the LORD, and after laying a hand on the head of the offering, it shall then be slaughtered before the tent of meeting. Aaron's sons shall splash its blood on all the sides of the altar. From the communion sacrifice the individual shall present as an oblation to the LORD its fat: the whole fatty tail, which is removed close to the spine, the fat that covers the inner organs, and all the fat that adheres to them, as well as the two kidneys, with the fat on them near the loins, and the lobe of the liver, which is removed with the kidneys. The priest shall burn this on the altar as food, an oblation to the LORD. If a person's offering is a goat, the individual shall bring it before the LORD, and after laying a hand on its head, it shall then be slaughtered before the tent of meeting. Aaron's sons shall splash its blood on all the sides of the altar. From this the one sacrificing shall present an offering as an oblation to the LORD: the fat that covers the inner organs, and all the fat that adheres to them, as well as the two kidneys, with the fat on them near the loins, and the lobe of the liver, which is removed with the kidneys. The priest shall burn these on the altar as food, a sweet-smelling oblation. All the fat belongs to the LORD. This shall be a perpetual ordinance for your descendants wherever they may dwell. You shall not eat any fat or any blood.

Deuteronomy 15:21 But if a firstling has any defect, lameness or blindness, any such serious defect, you shall not sacrifice it to the LORD, your God. (Old Testament/Covenant)

John the Baptist's Testimony to Jesus

John 1:29 "The next day he saw Jesus coming toward him and said, 'Behold, the Lamb of God, who takes away the sin of the world'" (New Testament/ Covenant).

The Last Supper, the Betrayal Foretold

Ultimate sacrifice offering (John 3:16–18) presented and reemphasized through three of the Gospel authors: Luke 22:14–19, Matthew 26:26–28, Mark 14:22–23 (New Testament/Covenant).

Luke 22:14–19 When the hour came, he took his place at table with the apostles. He said to them, *"I have eagerly desired to eat this Passover with you before I suffer, for, I tell you, I shall not eat it [again] until there is fulfillment in the kingdom of God."* Then he took a cup, gave thanks, and said, *"Take this and share it among yourselves; for I tell you [that] from this time on I shall not drink of the fruit of the vine until the kingdom of God comes."* Then he took the bread, said the blessing, broke it, and gave it to them, saying, *"This is my body, which will be given for you; do this in memory of me."* And likewise the cup after they had eaten, saying, *"This cup is the new covenant in my blood, which will be shed for you."*

Matthew 26:26–28 While they were eating, Jesus took bread, said the blessing, broke it, and giving it to his disciples said, *"Take and eat; this is my body."* Then he took a cup, gave thanks, and gave it to them, saying, *"Drink from it, all of you, for this is my blood of the covenant, which will be shed on behalf of many for the forgiveness of sins."*

Mark 14:22–24 While they were eating, he took bread, said the blessing, broke it, and gave it to them, and said, *"Take it; this is my body."* Then he took a cup, gave thanks, and gave it to them, and they all drank from it. He said to them, *"This is my blood of the covenant, which will be shed for many."*

Luke 22:21–23 *"And yet behold, the hand of the one who is to betray me is with me on the table; for the Son of Man indeed goes as it has been determined; but woe to that man by whom he is betrayed."* And they began to debate among themselves who among them would do such a deed.

Commentary

In this chapter I presented how the offerings to the Lord transitioned from the Old Testament, pre-Jesus Christ (Genesis, Leviticus, Deuteronomy), to the New Testament, Jesus Christ the body and blood offering (John, Luke, Matthew, Mark). It is interesting to me as it foretells the procession of the mass that has continued since

Jesus appeared to the disciples. In Acts 1:1–5, it mentions how Jesus "presented himself alive to them by many proofs after he had suffered [passed away], appearing to them during forty days and speaking about the kingdom of God." I can only imagine it was like an intense training session, like a sport's pre-season camp. I can imagine Jesus going over and over again the script of the mass; nope, do it again, do it again, do it again. In chapter 9 to come we'll see how Paul, twenty years later, goes back to the pre-season training. Paul teaches his followers to go back to the basics that Jesus taught of himself and the body and blood of Christ.

An interesting thought I picked up through lay formation: Do you know how to tell the ones who truly believe and know it is Jesus Christ versus those that may not have a clue? See how they take the host and watch what they do. Did they start walking away, then stop and turn toward the tabernacle or the cross to do the sign of the cross where the body of Christ resides? Therein lies the first hint to understanding what just happened. As Monsignor taught us, hello, Jesus just came into your hands, he just entered your body, and there is no need to stop and genuflect or give a sign of the cross back toward the tabernacle (ark of the covenant in Old Testament terms, a receptacle for the consecrated elements of the Eucharist). Jesus is in you—true body, blood, soul, and divinity of Christ. Take him in and walk away. Yes, you can do the sign of the cross as you're walking away, but understand you have just taken him and he is in you! Welcome him, shout with joy internally, and thank him for coming to you in the form he passed on to the apostles and the priests. Go back to your seat, don't run out the door (there's another hint), kneel if you can, know he is still with you and in you, talk to him, let him talk to you, and let him infuse into your body. Let him transform you from the person you are to the person he wants you to be. It will take time; sometimes it will take years. Look at me. I was a stubborn man, just as naïve, well into my forties, and I would have still been naive if I hadn't dedicated some time to learning.

I've heard stats indicating that 70 to 90 percent of Catholics do not believe in the true presence or body and blood of Christ. I would have to agree with that stat based on what is observed in the reception of the body and blood of Christ. Know the body and blood of Christ change you from the inside out. I like to make the comparison to a vitamin, the more and more you take in a vitamin, let's say iron, the more and more your iron level goes up. The same applies to the true body and blood of Christ.

Without fail, if you study *devout, true-believing* Catholics (Christians), what you are going to notice is they are devout to the "true presence," body, and blood of Christ. The body and blood are the epitome of the Mass. They are the primary reason why you don't want to miss Mass on Sundays. It is Christ's gift to humanity. Today, my recommendation is to go to Mass as often as you get a chance. The more you take him and his words in, the quicker you are going to experience the gifts he has in store for you.

Still don't believe? Think about this: Why did Paul, in the Bible, on his third journey back to Corinth, make it a point to reiterate the following to the Corinthians twenty-two years later (year AD 55 according to the introductory of the Corinthians)?

1 Corinthians 11:23–25
"For I received from the Lord what I also handed on to you, that the Lord Jesus, on the night he was handed over, took bread, and, after he had given thanks, broke it and said, *'This is my body that is for you. Do this in remembrance of me.'"*

JESUS THE THREAT/CRUCIFIXION

The Conspiracy against Jesus

Luke 22:1–6 Now the feast of Unleavened Bread, called the Passover, was drawing near, and the chief priests and the scribes were seeking a way to put him to death, for they were afraid of the people. Then Satan entered into Judas, the one surnamed Iscariot, who was counted among the Twelve, and he went to the chief priests and temple guards to discuss a plan for handing him over to them. They were pleased and agreed to pay him money. He accepted their offer and sought a favorable opportunity to hand him over to them in the absence of a crowd.

The Betrayal and Arrest of Jesus

Luke 22:47–53 While he was still speaking, a crowd approached and in front was one of the Twelve, a man named Judas. He went up to Jesus to kiss him. Jesus said to him, *"Judas, are you betraying the Son of Man with a kiss?"* His disciples realized what was about to happen, and they asked, "Lord, shall we strike with a sword?" And one of them struck the high priest's servant and cut off his right ear. But Jesus said in reply, *"Stop, no more of this!"* Then he touched the servant's ear and healed him. And Jesus said to the chief priests and temple guards and elders who had come for him, *"Have you come out as against a robber, with swords and clubs? Day after day I was with you in the temple area, and you did not seize me; but this is your hour, the time for the power of darkness."*

Jesus Before the Sanhedrin

Luke 22:66–71 When day came the council of elders of the people met, both chief priests and scribes, and they brought Jesus before their Sanhedrin. They said, "If you are the Messiah, tell us," but he replied to them, *"If I tell you, you will not believe, and if I question, you will not respond. But from this time on the Son of Man will be seated at the right hand of the power of God."* They all asked, "Are you then the Son of God?" He replied to them, *"You say that I am."* Then they said, "What further need have we for testimony? We have heard it from his own mouth."

The Inquiry before Annas

John 18:19–24 The high priest questioned Jesus about his disciples and about his doctrine. Jesus answered him, *"I have spoken publicly to the world. I have always taught in a synagogue or in the temple area where all the Jews gather, and in secret I have said nothing. Why ask me? Ask those who heard me what I said to them. They know what I said."* When he had said this, one of the temple guards standing there struck Jesus and said, "Is this the way you answer the high priest?" Jesus answered him, *"If I have spoken wrongly, testify to the wrong; but if I have spoken rightly, why do you strike me?"* Then Annas sent him bound to Caiaphas the high priest.

John 19:7 The Jews answered "We have a law, and according to that law he ought to die, because he made himself the Son of God."

Jesus before Pilate

Luke 23:1–5 Then the whole assembly of them arose and brought him before Pilate. They brought charges against him, saying, "We found this man misleading our people; he opposes the payment of taxes to Caesar and maintains that he is the Messiah, a king." Pilate asked him, "Are you the king of the Jews?" He said to him in reply, *"You say so."* Pilate then addressed the chief priests and the crowds, "I find this man not guilty." But they were adamant and said, "He is inciting the people with his teaching throughout all Judea, from Galilee where he began even to here."

Jesus before Herod

Luke 23:6–17 On hearing this Pilate asked if the man was a Galilean; and upon learning that he was under Herod's jurisdiction, he sent him to Herod who was in Jerusalem at that time. Herod was very glad to see Jesus; he had been wanting to see him for a long time, for he had heard about him and had been hoping to see him perform some sign. He questioned him at length, but he gave him no answer. The chief priests and scribes, meanwhile, stood by accusing him harshly. [Even] Herod and his soldiers treated him contemptuously and mocked him, and after clothing him in resplendent garb, he sent him back to Pilate.

Herod and Pilate became friends that very day, even though they had been enemies formerly. Pilate then summoned the chief priests, the rulers, and the people and said to them, "You brought this man to me and accused him of inciting the people to revolt. I have conducted my investigation in your presence and have not found this man guilty of the charges you have brought against him, nor did Herod, for he sent him back to us. So no capital crime has been committed by him. Therefore, I shall have him flogged and then release him."

The Sentence of Death

Luke 23:18–25 But all together they shouted out, "Away with this man! Release Barabbas to us." [Now Barabbas had been imprisoned for a rebellion that had taken place in the city and for murder]. Again, Pilate addressed them, still wishing to release Jesus, but they continued their shouting, "Crucify him! Crucify him!" Pilate addressed them a third time, "What evil has this man done? I found him guilty of no capital crime. Therefore, I shall have him flogged and then release him." With loud shouts, however, they persisted in calling for his crucifixion, and their voices prevailed. The verdict of Pilate was that their demand should be granted. So he released the man who had been imprisoned for rebellion and murder, for whom they asked, and he handed Jesus over to them to deal with as they wished.

The Crucifixion

Luke 23:33–43 When they came to the place called the Skull, they crucified him and the criminals there, one on his right, the other on his left. Then Jesus said, *"Father, forgive them, they know not what they do."* They divided his garments by casting lots. The people stood by and watched; the rulers, meanwhile, sneered at him and said, "He saved others, let him save himself if he is the chosen one, the Messiah of God." Even the soldiers jeered at him. As they approached to offer him wine they called out, "If you are King of the Jews, save yourself." Above him there was an inscription that read, "This is the King of the Jews." Now one of the criminals hanging there reviled Jesus, saying, "Are you not the Messiah? Save yourself and us." The other, however, rebuking him, said in reply, "Have you no fear of God, for you are subject to the same condemnation? And indeed, we have been condemned justly, for the sentence we received corresponds to our crimes, but this man has done nothing criminal." Then he said, "Jesus, remember me when you come into your kingdom." He replied to him, *"Amen, I say to you, today you will be with me in Paradise."*

Psalm 116:5

Gracious is the LORD and righteous; yes, our God is merciful.

The Death of Jesus

Luke 23:44–49 It was now about noon and darkness came over the whole land until three in the afternoon because of an eclipse of the sun. Then the veil of the temple was torn down the middle. Jesus cried out in a loud voice, *"Father, into your hands I commend my spirit"*; and when he had said this he breathed his last. The centurion who witnessed what had happened glorified God and said, "This man was innocent beyond doubt." When all the people who had gathered for this spectacle saw what had happened, they returned home beating their breasts; but all his acquaintances stood at a distance, including the women who had followed him from Galilee and saw these events.

The Burial of Jesus

Luke 23:50–53 Now there was a virtuous and righteous man named Joseph who, though he was a member of the council, had not consented to their plan of action. He came from the Jewish town of Arimathea and was awaiting the kingdom of God. He went to Pilate and asked for the body of Jesus. After he had taken the body down, he wrapped it in a linen cloth and laid him in a rock-hewn tomb in which no one had yet been buried.

Commentary

In this chapter we walk with Jesus as he is tried and crucified. Despite Pilot and Herod not being able to find any "capital crime" against Jesus, Pilot commits him to be "flogged and then released." This chapter is very interesting to study as the entire tide turns on Jesus and he simply goes with it. This chapter (the passion of Christ) is repeated every year through holy week as practically all the Christian churches around the globe remember and reenact the crucifixion as Jesus's resurrection (rising) nears (Easter). As has been mentioned coming into this chapter, he knew his mission and he accepted it. Thanks to his acceptance we are accepted by God (John 3:16).

He is risen! Rejoice and be glad!

PAUL'S LETTER TO THE CORINTHIANS

Paul established a Christian community in Corinth about the year 51 (after Christ). On his second missionary journey, he responds both to questions addressed to him and to situations of which he had been informed (New Testament).

1 Corinthians 11:23–27 For I received from the Lord what I also handed on to you, that the Lord Jesus, on the night he was handed over, took bread, and, after he had given thanks, broke it and said, *"This is my body that is for you. Do this in remembrance of me…"* In the same way also the cup, after supper, saying, *"This cup is the new covenant in my blood. Do this, as often as you drink it, in remembrance of me."* For as often as you eat this bread and drink the cup, you proclaim the death of the Lord until he comes. Therefore, whoever eats the bread or drinks the cup of the Lord unworthily will have to answer for the body and blood of the Lord [Reason for the book *John 3:16.5: The Rest of the Story*].

Commentary from Saint Cyril of Alexandria (380–444), Bishop, Doctor of the Church

They have inherited blessings impossible to express or comprehend, for "eye has not seen," says Scripture, "nor ear heard, nor human heart conceived what God has prepared for those who love him" (1 Corinthians 2:9).

One Body, Many Parts

1 Corinthians 12:12–26 *(New Testament, twenty years after Christ's death)* As a body is one though it has many parts, and all the parts of the body, though many, are one body, so also Christ. For in one Spirit we were all baptized into one body, whether Jews or Greeks, slaves or free persons, and we were all given to drink of one Spirit. Now the body is not a single part, but many. If a foot should say, "Because I am not a hand I do not belong to the body," it does not for this reason belong any less to the body. Or if an ear should say, "Because I am not an eye I do not belong to the body," it does not for this reason belong any less to the body. If the whole body were an eye, where would the hearing be? If the whole body were hearing, where would the sense of smell be? But as it is, God placed the parts, each one of them, in the body as he intended. If they were all one part, where would the body be? But as it is, there are many parts, yet one body. The eye cannot say to the hand, "I do not need you," nor again the head to the feet, "I do not need you." Indeed, the parts of the body that seem to be weaker are all the more necessary, and those parts of the body that we consider less honorable we surround with greater honor, and our less presentable parts are treated with greater propriety, whereas our more presentable parts do not need this. But God has so constructed the body as to give greater honor to a part

that is without it, so that there may be no division in the body, but that the parts may have the same concern for one another. If [one] part suffers, all the parts suffer with it; if one part is honored, all the parts share its joy.

Application to Christ

1 Corinthians 12:27–30 Now you are Christ's body, and individually parts of it. Some people God has designated in the church to be first, apostles; second, prophets; third, teachers; then, mighty deeds; then, gifts of healing, assistance, administration, and varieties of tongues. Are all apostles? No. Are all prophets? No. Are all teachers? No. Do all work mighty deeds? No. Do all have gifts of healing? No. Do all speak in tongues? No. Do all interpret? No.

I am reminding you, brothers and sisters, of the Gospel I preached to you, which you indeed received and in which you also stand. Through it you are also being saved, if you hold fast to the word I preached to you, unless you believed in vain. For I handed on to you as of first importance what I also received: that Christ died for our sins in accordance with the scriptures; that he was buried; that he was raised on the third day in accordance with the scriptures; that he appeared to Kephas, then to the Twelve. After that, he appeared to more than five hundred brothers at once, most of whom are still living, though some have fallen asleep. After that he appeared to James, then to all the apostles. Last of all, as to one born abnormally, he appeared to me. For I am the least of the apostles, not fit to be called an apostle, because I persecuted the church of God. But by the grace of God, I am what I am, and his grace to me has not been ineffective. Indeed, I have toiled harder than all of them; not I, however, but the grace of God [that is] with me. Therefore, whether it be I or they, so we preach and so you believed.

Commentary

In this chapter (New Testament, post-Jesus), Paul shares with us what he learned and experienced under the teachings of Jesus. The thing that sticks out is this is years after Jesus passed away. Paul unites the community of Corinth as it begins to meander and reminds the congregation to the unity and body of the church as one. Interesting and as further proof to the unity and structure of the church, Paul is challenged by the congregation on the Old Testament tradition of circumcision. Paul returns to Peter in Jerusalem and the first council of the church has had (first council of Jerusalem). The one decision comes out, and it is disseminated in the same structured and orderly fashion as the church conducts itself today.

The Life That the Lord Has Assigned

1 Corinthians 7:17–20 Only, everyone should live as the Lord has assigned, just as God called each one. I give this order in all the churches. Was someone called after he had been circumcised? He should not try to undo his circumcision. Was an uncircumcised person called? He should not be circumcised. Circumcision means nothing, and uncircumcision means nothing; what matters is keeping God's commandments. Everyone should remain in the state in which he was called.

Know there are multiple interpretations and discernments to the question of circumcision. One interpretation says we *circumcise* ourselves (fast) to the worldly ways and things.

MASS CELEBRATION AS REVEALED THROUGH SCRIPTURE
(Old and New Testament)

Ezra Reads the Law

Nehemiah 8:1–10 *(Old Testament/Before Christ)* Now when the seventh month came, the whole people gathered as one in the square in front of the Water Gate, and they called upon Ezra the scribe to bring forth the book of the law of Moses which the LORD had commanded for Israel. On the first day of the seventh month, therefore, Ezra the priest brought the law before the assembly, which consisted of men, women, and those children old enough to understand. In the square in front of the Water Gate, Ezra read out of the book from daybreak till midday, in the presence of the men, the women, and those children old enough to understand; and all the people listened attentively to the book of the law.

Ezra the scribe stood on a wooden platform that had been made for the occasion; at his right side stood Mattithiah, Shema, Anaiah, Uriah, Hilkiah, and

Maaseiah, and on his left Pedaiah, Mishael, Malchijah, Hashum, Hashbaddanah, Zechariah, Meshullam.

Ezra opened the scroll so that all the people might see it, for he was standing higher than any of the people.

When he opened it, all the people stood. Ezra blessed the LORD, the great God, and all the people, their hands raised high, answered, "Amen, amen!"

Then they knelt down and bowed before the LORD, their faces to the ground. The Levites Jeshua, Bani, Sherebiah, Jamin, Akkub, Shabbethai, Hodiah, Maaseiah, Kelita, Azariah, Jozabad, Hanan, and Pelaiah explained the law to the people, who remained in their places. Ezra read clearly from the book of the law of God, interpreting it so that all could understand what was read.

Then Nehemiah, that is, the governor, and Ezra the priest-scribe, and the Levites who were instructing the people said to all the people: "Today is holy to the LORD your God. Do not lament, do not weep!"—for all the people were weeping as they heard the words of the law. He continued: "Go, eat rich foods and drink sweet drinks, and allot portions to those who had nothing prepared; for today is holy to our LORD. Do not be saddened this day, for rejoicing in the LORD is your strength!"

Deuteronomy 26:4–11 Then the priest shall take the basket from your hand and set it down before the altar of the LORD your God. "And you shall make response before the LORD your God, 'A wandering Aramean was my father. And he went down into Egypt and sojourned there, few in number, and there he became a nation, great, mighty, and populous. And the Egyptians treated us harshly and humiliated us and laid on us hard labor. Then we cried to the LORD, the God of our fathers, and the LORD heard our voice and saw our affliction, our toil, and our oppression. And the LORD brought us out of Egypt with a mighty hand and an outstretched arm, with great deeds of terror, with signs and wonders. And he brought us into this place and gave us this land, a land flowing with milk and honey. And behold, now I bring the first of the fruit of the ground, which you, O LORD, have given me.' And you shall set it down before the LORD your God and worship before the LORD your God. And you shall rejoice in all the good that the LORD your God has given to you and to your house, you, and the Levite, and the sojourner who is among you.

Luke 1:1–4 *(New Testament)* Since many have undertaken to compile a narrative of the events that have been fulfilled among us, just as those who were eyewitnesses from the beginning and ministers of the word have handed them down to us, too have decided, after investigating everything accurately anew, to write it down in an orderly sequence for you, most excellent Theophilus, so that you may realize the certainty of the teachings you have received.

The Beginning of the Galilean Ministry

Luke 4:14–15 Jesus returned to Galilee in the power of the Spirit, and news of him spread throughout the whole region. He taught in their synagogues and was praised by all.

The Rejection at Nazareth

Luke 4:16–21 He came to Nazareth, where he had grown up, and went according to his custom into the synagogue on the sabbath day. He stood up to read and was handed a scroll of the prophet Isaiah. He unrolled the scroll and found the passage where it was written: "The Spirit of the Lord is upon me, because he has anointed me to bring glad tidings to the poor. He has sent me to proclaim liberty to captives and recovery of sight to the blind, to let the oppressed go free, and to proclaim a year acceptable to the Lord." Rolling up the scroll, he handed it back to the attendant and sat down, and the eyes of all in the synagogue looked intently at him. He said to them, *"Today this scripture passage is fulfilled in your hearing."*

Commentary Given by Priest and Theologian Origen (c.185–253)

When you read that "He taught in their synagogues and everyone praised him," take care not to consider Christ's listeners to be blessed and to think of yourselves as deprived of his teaching. If Scripture is true, then God did not just speak in former times in the meeting places of the Jews, but he still speaks today in our own assemblies. And not just here, in our own assembly, but in other meeting places. And all over the world Jesus teaches and seeks out bearers of his Word to pass on his teaching. Pray that he may find me both ready and able to sing it.

Just as Almighty God, seeking for prophets at a time when prophecy was lacking to men, finds Isaiah, Jeremiah, Ezekiel, Daniel, for example, so Jesus seeks out bearers of the message to pass on his Word, to "teach in their synagogues and be praised by all." Today Jesus is even more "praised by all" than at the time when he was only known in a single province.

In the introduction of the book I mentioned, I didn't even know we were reading the Bible. Deacon Frank thought it would be good to give a clip on the fact that we do read the Bible each and every day.

In short there are "three seasons" of the church. The church liturgical (liturgy/readings) year always begins in December with advent where we cover the coming of Jesus Christ (Christmas,

December 25, Jesus Christ's celebrated birthday—Christmas). The next season that usually begins in February is lent. Lent begins on Ash Wednesday. Through lent we are reading and leading to the coming of Jesus death on Good Friday. We celebrate his resurrection (our salvation) on Easter Sunday. Something few Christians celebrate is the Easter season. The Easter season actually begins on Easter, and it traditionally goes out fifty days when we celebrate Pentecost (penta meaning fifty). During Pentecost Sunday we hear of the release of the Holy Spirit by Jesus "in the upper room." The last season is actually the times spent between the seasons, and you'll hear "ordinary time."

Concluding: The church does cover 50 percent of the Bible via its daily and Sunday masses every three years. The way it rhythmically and methodically shifts and runs from one year to the other (December to November of the following year) is via the gospels of St. Matthew (A), St. Mark (B), and St. Luke (C). Every year, for three years, the readings are coming from the A, B, or C cyclical year reading. In three years, after you have gone through the three books, half the Bible has been read.

While the daily mass is not a "holy day of obligation," Sunday is a "holy day of obligation." The six holy days of obligation, other than Sundays, on which Americans celebrate the great things God has done for us are:

> January 1—Mary, mother of God
> Fortieth day after Easter—Ascension
> August 15—Assumption of the Blessed Virgin Mary
> November 1—All Saints
> December 8—Immaculate Conception
> December 25—Nativity of our Lord Jesus Christ

After thought, notice how Ash Wednesday is *not* mentioned as one of the holy days of obligation, yet it is one of the most attended masses in the year (worldwide).

I encourage you to go to a daily mass or just pop in to a church one day. I'll never forget the first time I went into a church with no intentions, during the week, just to pray, on my own. It was the year

2000. Our second child, Elisa, had just been born that year. With her birth, I decided I wanted to do more. I didn't feel I was doing what I was called to do. I requested and was approved a whole year's leave without pay from my federal job. I started my own home inspection business, and basically it took some work. I don't think I went in to pray for anything in particular, but I'm sure I probably prayed to God for his accompaniment and support that year. I remember I finished doing some marketing leg work, and I passed by the church and I wondered if it's open. I circled back, and sure enough it was open. I remember it like the scene on *Sixteen Candles*, where the guy pulls up to the church and his car is centered up to the white church and no one else is there. Anyhow, I went in, kneeled, prayed, sat there, and basically took a breather; it was so good (no worries). At the time, I was so novice, I didn't even know I had performed the act of *adoration* toward our Lord that was in the tabernacle (the golden box or housing where our Lord resides, up front behind the altar).

Today, when I feel the calling, I go to adoration or daily mass when I feel like it. I won't say I go often, but I guess I can say I do go regularly when I just need to go be with someone, my friend—him.

May God bless you and may you be a blessing to all the people God presents to you, every single day. I'll leave you with one of Msgr. Hera's favorite marque quotes on the Bible and Christianity:

"Silence is golden, sometimes it's yellow."

Don't be yellow when it comes to speaking up for our God.

I mentioned at the very beginning of the book under the acknowledgments that Deacon Frank would be submitting a detailed contribution on the mass. The following information was handed to me by Deacon Frank. Apparently, this information was way above his head too as he provided it to me from an article posted in the *United States Conference of Catholic Bishops*. Just kidding, people. Lighten up, God's people! Why work harder if we can work smarter? Never forget, as Deacon provides, we are many parts yet one body. Utilize your approved, authorized resources!

The Structure and Meaning of the Mass
(Reference the appendix for a link to the
Structure and Meaning of the Mass.)

Introductory Rites

The Mass begins with the entrance song. The celebrant and other ministers enter in procession and reverence the altar with a bow and/or a kiss. The altar is a symbol of Christ at the heart of the assembly and so deserves this special reverence.

All make the Sign of the Cross and the celebrant extends a greeting to the gathered people in words taken from Scripture.

The Act of Penitence. At the very beginning of the Mass, the faithful recall their sins and place their trust in God's abiding mercy.

On Sundays and solemnities, the *Gloria* follows the Act of Penitence. The *Gloria* begins by echoing the song of the angels at the birth of Christ: "Glory to God in the highest!" In this ancient hymn, the gathered assembly joins the heavenly choirs in offering praise and adoration to the Father and Jesus through the Holy Spirit.

Liturgy of the Word

Most of the Liturgy of the Word is made up of readings from Scripture.

In the Liturgy of the Word, the Church feeds the people of God from the table of his Word (cf. *Constitution on the Sacred Liturgy*, no. 51). The Scriptures are the word of God, written under the inspiration of the Holy Spirit. In the Scriptures, God speaks to us, leading us along the path to salvation.

The high point of the Liturgy of the Word is the reading of the Gospel. Because the Gospels tell of the life, ministry, and preaching of Christ, it receives several special signs of honor and reverence. The gathered assembly stands to hear the Gospel

During most of the year, that acclamation is "Alleluia!" derived from a Hebrew phrase meaning "Praise the Lord!" A deacon (or, if no deacon is present, a priest) reads the Gospel.

After the Scripture readings, the celebrant preaches the homily. In the homily, the preacher focuses on the Scripture texts or some other texts from the liturgy, drawing from them lessons that may help us to live better lives, more faithful to Christ's call to grow in holiness.

In many Masses, the Nicene Creed follows the homily. The Nicene Creed is a statement of faith dating from the fourth century. In certain instances, the Nicene Creed may be replaced by the Apostles' Creed (the ancient baptismal creed of the Church in Rome) or by a renewal of baptismal promises, based on the Apostles' Creed. Links provided for those reading the hard book:

Nicene Creed—https://www.usccb.org/beliefs-and-teachings/what-we-believe

Apostles' Creed—https://www.usccb.org/prayers/apostles-creed

The United States Conference of Catholic Bishops' (USCCB's)

Liturgy of the Eucharist

The Liturgy of the Eucharist begins with the preparation of the gifts and the altar. As the ministers prepare the altar, representatives of the people bring forward the bread and wine that will become the Body and Blood of Christ. The celebrant blesses and praises God for these gifts and places them on the altar. In addition to the bread and wine, monetary gifts for the support of the Church and the care of the poor may be brought forward [the tithe].

The next major part of the Eucharistic Prayer is the *epiclesis*. In the *epiclesis*, the priest asks the Father to send the Holy Spirit on the gifts of bread and wine so that, through the power of the Spirit, they may become the Body and Blood of Christ. This same Spirit will transform those attending the liturgy that they may grow in their unity with each other, with the whole Church, and with Christ.

The Eucharistic Prayer continues with the *anamnesis*, literally, the "not forgetting." The people proclaim the memorial acclamation, recalling the saving death and resurrection of the Lord. The prayer continues as the celebrant recalls the saving actions of God in Christ.

The Eucharistic Prayer concludes with the Final Doxology. The celebrant makes the prayer through, in, and with Jesus, in union with the Holy Spirit, and presents it to God the Father. The people respond with the Great Amen, a joyous affirmation of their faith and participation in this great sacrifice of praise.

Before receiving Communion, the celebrant and assembly acknowledge that we are unworthy to receive so great a gift. The celebrant receives Communion first and then the people come forward.

Those who receive Communion should be prepared to receive so great a gift. They should fast (except for medicines) for one hour before receiving the Eucharist and should not be conscious of having committed serious sin.

Because sharing at the Eucharistic Table is a sign of unity in the Body of Christ, only Catholics [in complete union with the Church's beliefs and in clean conscience [reconciliation]] may receive Communion. To invite all present to receive Communion implies a unity which really does not exist.

Those who do not receive Communion still participate in this rite by praying from their pews [seats or kneeling] for unity with Christ and with each other.

The people approach the altar and, bowing with reverence, receive Communion. People may receive the Body of Christ either on the tongue or in the hand. The priest or other minister offers the Eucharist to each person saying, "The Body of Christ." The person receiving responds by saying, "Amen," a Hebrew word meaning, "So be it" (*Catechism of the Catholic Church*, 2856).

As the people receive Communion, the communion song is sung. The unity of voices echoes the unity the Eucharist brings. All may spend some time in silent prayer of thanksgiving as well.

The Communion Rite ends with the Prayer after Communion which asks that the benefits of the Eucharist will remain active in our daily lives.

Concluding Rites

When it is necessary, announcements may be made. The celebrant then blesses the people assembled. In every case, the blessing always concludes "in the name of the Father, and of the Son, and of the Holy Spirit." It is in the triune God and in the sign of the cross that we find our blessing.

After the blessing, the deacon dismisses the people. In fact, the dismissal gives the liturgy its name. The word "Mass" comes from the Latin word, *"Missa."* At one time, the people were dismissed with the words *"Ite, missa est,"* meaning "Go, you are sent." The word *"Missa"* comes from the word *"missio,"* the root of the English word "mission." The liturgy does not simply come to an end. Those assembled are sent forth to bring the fruits of the Eucharist to the world.

If you are reading this excerpt of the article in the book and if you wish to read the article in its entirety, please google "The Structure and Meaning of the Mass." Source: United States Conference of Catholic Bishops (USCCB).

CLASSIC BONUS READS

The Parable of the Lost Son or Better Known as the Prodigal Son

Luke 15:11–32 Then he said, "A man had two sons, and the younger son said to his father, 'Father, give me the share of your estate that should come to me.' So the father divided the property between them. After a few days, the younger son collected all his belongings and set off to a distant country where he squandered his inheritance on a life of dissipation. When he had freely spent everything, a severe famine struck that country, and he found himself in dire need. So he hired himself out to one of the local citizens who sent him to his farm to tend the swine. And he longed to eat his fill of the pods on which the swine fed, but nobody gave him any. Coming to his senses he thought, 'How many of my father's hired workers have more than enough food to eat, but here am I, dying from hunger. I shall get up and go to my father and I shall say to him, "Father, I have sinned against heaven and against you. I no longer deserve to be called your son; treat me as you would treat one of your hired workers." So he got up and went back to his father. While he was still a long way off, his father caught sight of him, and was filled with compassion. He ran to his son, embraced him and kissed him. His son said to him, 'Father, I have sinned against heaven and against you; I no longer deserve to be called your son.' But his father ordered his servants, 'Quickly bring the finest robe and put it on him; put a ring on his finger and sandals on his feet. Take the fattened calf and slaughter it. Then let us celebrate with a feast, because this son of mine was dead, and has come to life again; he was lost, and has been found.' Then the celebration began. Now the older son had been out in the field and, on his way back, as he neared the house, he heard the sound of music and dancing. He called one of the servants and asked what this might mean. The servant said to him, 'Your brother has returned and your father has slaughtered the fattened calf because he has him back safe and sound.' He became angry, and when he refused to enter the house, his father came out and pleaded with him. He said to his father in reply, 'Look, all these years I served you and not once did I disobey your orders; yet you never gave me even a young goat to feast on with my friends. But when your son returns who swallowed up your property with prostitutes, for him you slaughter the fattened calf.' He said to him, 'My son, you are here with me always; everything I have is yours. But now we must celebrate and rejoice, because your brother was dead and has come to life again; he was lost and has been found.'"

Narration

"The Prodigal Son" is classic Christian read of three characters that exemplify the challenges, stresses, and evolution of life. The two sons represent God's children as we go through ups and downs in life. On the first hand, the *prodigal son* exemplifies human nature of wanting it all and losing it all as we pursue life on our terms. The *second brother* exemplifies the person that while he chooses to abide and have it all he is tested to his father's love for the prodigal son that comes back. The father portrays our Father in heaven himself, ever patient, waiting, gracious, loving toward all his children.

Beatitudes—The Sermon on the Mount

Matthew 5:1–12 When he saw the crowds, he went up
the mountain, and after he had sat down, his disciples
came to him. He began to teach them, saying:
Blessed are the poor in spirit, for theirs is the kingdom of heaven.
Blessed are they who mourn, for they will be comforted.
Blessed are the meek, for they will inherit the land.
Blessed are they who hunger and thirst for
righteousness, for they will be satisfied.
Blessed are the merciful, for they will be shown mercy.
Blessed are the clean of heart, for they will see God.
Blessed are the peacemakers, for they will be called children of God.
Blessed are they who are persecuted for the sake of
righteousness, for theirs is the kingdom of heaven.
Blessed are you when they insult you and persecute you and
utter every kind of evil against you [falsely] because of me.
Rejoice and be glad, for your reward will be great in heaven.
Thus, they persecuted the prophets who were before you.

Narration

When I was young, maybe five to six years old, I remember a song we sang repeatedly one summer Bible school year: "Whatsoever you do, to the least of my brothers, that you do unto me." I loved how this song, after a long hot day in the sun playing, would lull me into an intangible bliss or restful afternoon in the air-conditioned church. What I liked about the song was it was so simple and peaceful like a balloon floating into the sky. "The Beatitudes" is a similar read that gives us a good image into the Christian as we ponder life after death. While much of the secular world focuses on the immediate tangible rewards, Christianity presents to us the greater or eternal intangible rewards that last beyond life on earth. When we reflect on the peace that comes from just sitting and listening to someone or something, the wind or just gazing at the rising or setting sun, we realize there's got to be something greater in life.

The Ten Commandments

Exodus 20:1–17 Then God spoke all these words: I am the LORD your God, who brought you out of the land of Egypt, out of the house of slavery. You shall not have other gods beside me. You shall not make for yourself an idol or a likeness of anything in the heavens above or on the earth below or in the waters beneath the earth; you shall not bow down before them or serve them. For I, the LORD, your God, am a jealous God, inflicting punishment for their ancestors' wickedness on the children of those who hate me, down to the third and fourth generation; but showing love down to the thousandth generation of those who love me and keep my commandments. You shall not invoke the name of the LORD, your God, in vain. For the LORD will not leave unpunished anyone who invokes his name in vain. Remember the sabbath day—keep it holy. Six days you may labor and do all your work, but the seventh day is a sabbath of the LORD your God. You shall not do any work, either you, your son or your daughter, your male or female slave, your work animal, or the resident alien within your gates. For in six days the LORD made the heavens and the earth, the sea and all that is in them; but on the seventh day he rested. That is why the LORD has blessed the sabbath day and made it holy. Honor your father and your mother, that you may have a long life in the land the LORD your God is giving you. You shall not kill. You shall not commit adultery. You shall not steal. You shall not bear false witness against your neighbor. You shall not covet your neighbor's house. You shall not covet your neighbor's wife, his male or female slave, his ox or donkey, or anything that belongs to your neighbor.

The Greatest Commandment

John 22:34–40 When the Pharisees heard that he had silenced the Sadducees, they gathered together, and one of them [a scholar of the law] tested him by asking, "Teacher, which commandment in the law is the greatest?" He said to him, "You shall love the Lord, your God, with all your heart, with all your soul, and with all your mind. This is the greatest and the first commandment. The second is like it: You shall love your neighbor as yourself. The whole law and the prophets depend on these two commandments."

Narration

I thought it was good to present the Ten Commandments in this book. While they are first introduced to us in the Old Testament (Exodus), Jesus speaks to them in the New Testament. Matthew 5:17, "Do not think that I have come to abolish the law or the prophets. I have come not to abolish but to fulfill." Something that was revealed to me was if you focus on the first four commandments, they are on how we are to treat and love our God. The final six commandments focus on how we treat and love our neighbor. If we focus on the first ten commandments faith, hope, and love rise, these three; but the greatest according to our Savior himself is love.

The Parable of the Ten Virgins

Matthew 25:1–13 Then the kingdom of heaven will be like ten virgins who took their lamps and went out to meet the bridegroom. Five of them were foolish and five were wise. The foolish ones, when taking their lamps, brought no oil with them, but the wise brought flasks of oil with their lamps. Since the bridegroom was long delayed, they all became drowsy and fell asleep. At midnight, there was a cry, "Behold, the bridegroom! Come out to meet him!" Then all those virgins got up and trimmed their lamps. The foolish ones said to the wise, "Give us some of your oil, for our lamps are going out." But the wise ones replied, "No, for there may not be enough for us and you. Go instead to the merchants and buy some for yourselves." While they went off to buy it, the bridegroom came and those who were ready went into the wedding feast with him. Then the door was locked. Afterwards the other virgins came and said, "Lord, Lord, open the door for us!" But he said in reply, "Amen, I say to you, I do not know you." Therefore, stay awake, for you know neither the day nor the hour.

The Parable of the Talents

Matthew 25:14–30 "It will be as when a man who was going on a journey called in his servants and entrusted his possessions to them. To one he gave five talents; to another, two; to a third, one—to each according to his ability. Then he went away. Immediately the one who received five talents went and traded with them, and made another five. Likewise, the one who received two made another two. But the man who received one went off and dug a hole in the ground and buried his master's money. After a long time, the master of those servants came back and settled accounts with them. The one who had received five talents came forward bringing the additional five. He said, 'Master, you gave me five talents. See, I have made five more.' His master said to him, 'Well done, my good and faithful servant. Since you were faithful in small matters, I will give you great responsibilities. Come, share your master's joy.' [Then] the one who had received two talents also came forward and said, 'Master, you gave me two talents. See, I have made two more.' His master said to him, 'Well done, my good and faithful servant. Since you were faithful in small matters, I will give you great responsibilities. Come, share your master's joy.' Then the one who had received the one talent came forward and said, 'Master, I knew you were a demanding person, harvesting where you did not plant and gathering where you did not scatter; so out of fear I went off and buried your talent in the ground. Here it is back.' His master said to him in reply, 'You wicked, lazy servant! So you knew that I harvest where I did not plant and gather where I did not scatter? Should you not then have put my money in the bank so that I could have got it back with interest on my return? Now then! Take the talent from him and give it to the one with ten. For to everyone who has, more will be given and he will grow rich; but from the one who has not, even what he has will be taken away. And throw this useless servant into the darkness outside, where there will be wailing and grinding of teeth.'

The Judgment of the Nations

Matthew 25:31–46 "When the Son of Man comes in his glory, and all the angels with him, he will sit upon his glorious throne, and all the nations will be assembled before him. And he will separate them one from another, as a shepherd separates the sheep from the goats. He will place the sheep on his right and the goats on his left. Then the king will say to those on his right, 'Come, you who are blessed by my Father. Inherit the kingdom prepared for you from the foundation of the world. For I was hungry and you gave me food, I was thirsty and you gave me drink, a stranger and you welcomed me, naked and you clothed me, ill and you cared for me, in prison and you visited me.' Then the righteous will answer him and say, 'Lord, when did we see you hungry and feed you, or thirsty and give you drink? When did we see you a stranger and welcome you, or naked and clothe you? When did we see you ill or in prison, and visit you?' And the king will say to them in reply, 'Amen, I say to you, whatever you did for one of these least brothers of mine, you did for me.' Then he will say to those on his left, 'Depart from me, you accursed, into the eternal fire prepared for the devil and his angels. For I was hungry and you gave me no food, I was thirsty and you gave me no drink, stranger and you gave me no welcome, naked and you gave me no clothing, ill and in prison, and you did not care for me.' Then they will answer and say, 'Lord, when did we see you hungry or thirsty or a stranger or naked or ill or in prison, and not minister to your needs?' He will answer them, 'Amen, I say to you, what you did not do for one of these least ones, you did not do for me.' And these will go off to eternal punishment, but the righteous to eternal life."

Matthew 25: The Diamond of the Rough

By far in my opinion (IMO), the best book and chapter of all the Bible is Matthew 25. I like to refer people to this book if they're questioning God's love or dismissing it. Matthew 25 wraps nicely *John 3:16.5*. While yes, God gave us his only Son, that we might have eternal life. When we take in the fullness of *the rest of the story*, then we begin to understand the *depths* of Christ's love and desires for each and every person, place, and thing in his created world. While our God is stern, he's ever so patient, loving, and receptive. Prodigal son, the adulterous Paul (a vigilant prosecutor of the church) are all great examples of where God (the church in the case of Paul) knew what was wrong, but still he (the church) welcomed them.

John 8:10–11
Then Jesus straightened up and said to her, "Woman,
where are they? Has no one condemned you?" She replied,
"No one, sir." Then Jesus said, "Neither do I condemn
you. Go, [and] from now on do not sin any more.

My prayer for you is to be God's light. Jesus counts on everyone.
"Be imitators of God, as beloved children and live in love, as Christ
loved us and handed himself over for us as a sacrificial offering to
God for a fragrant aroma" (Ephesians 5:1–2).

Parable of the Lamp

Mark 4:21–25 He said to them, "Is a lamp brought
in to be placed under a bushel basket or under a bed,
and not to be placed on a lampstand? For there is nothing hidden except to be made visible; nothing is secret
except to come to light. Anyone who has ears to hear
ought to hear." He also told them, "Take care what you
hear. The measure with which you measure will be mea-
sured out to you, and still more will be given to you. To
the one who has, more will be given; from the one who
has not, even what he has will be taken away."

The Return of the Twelve and the Feeding of the Five Thousand

Luke 9:10–17 When the apostles returned, they
explained to him what they had done. He took them
and withdrew in private to a town called Bethsaida. The
crowds, meanwhile, learned of this and followed him.
He received them and spoke to them about the kingdom of God, and he healed those who needed to be
cured. As the day was drawing to a close, the Twelve
approached him and said, "Dismiss the crowd so that
they can go to the surrounding villages and farms and
find lodging and provisions; for we are in a deserted

place here." He said to them, "Give them some food yourselves." They replied, "Five loaves and two fish are all we have, unless we ourselves go and buy food for all these people." Now the men there numbered about five thousand. Then he said to his disciples, "Have them sit down in groups of [about] fifty." They did so and made them all sit down. Then taking the five loaves and the two fish, and looking up to heaven, he said the blessing over them, broke them, and gave them to the disciples to set before the crowd. They all ate and were satisfied. And when the leftover fragments were picked up, they filled twelve wicker baskets.

Stop/Alto, Be Alert, Do the Work, Go Deeper

Something I wanted to bring to light in this book was the numbers and colors (bells, smells of the mass). Why do Christians do what they do and where did they get these things from? Most of the things came from the Bible, but many are natural fits that put the mind and body in the motion and mood of the occasion.

In this last Bible reading, we hear of Jesus and the miracle that he performed feeding five thousand people with the start of only *five* loaves and *two* fish. If you google biblical or spiritual meanings to numbers you will find there are meanings to practically everything. If you follow the numbers throughout the Bible you'll start hearing and seeing the repeated references in the interpretations. With time you'll start connecting numbers to references that give us a deeper meaning.

I did a quick google on what does the number 5 represent spiritually. The following is one of the interpretations that was returned. In numerology, the number 5 represents spiritual growth and self-confidence. In this story, we begin to see the spiritual growth being gained by the apostles.

What does 2 represent spiritually? The number 2 is a representation of harmony, kinship, and cooperation. As Jesus readies to leave earth this story from the Bible begins to illuminate the essence of harmony and cooperation in a church (a community, notice the *unity* in community).

The sum of five plus two gives us seven. What does 7 represent spiritually? "In Scripture, seven often symbolizes completion or perfection." While the apostles like the church will never be *perfect*, they are God's gift to us as I see it.

Why is the number 12 significant in the Bible? The number 12 is mentioned often in the New Testament of the Bible, such as Jesus's selection of twelve apostles. That choice was deliberate, with each apostle representing one of the twelve tribes of Israel, said Reed, a professor emeritus of pastoral theology and research. Notice how in the story the narrative begins with the twelve apostles and ends with twelve baskets, as if leaving the door open for the next hypothetical chapter. Go out and make fishers of men.

What can we learn from Jesus feeding the five thousand? Our human nature is to always think we need more to do more, but the story of Jesus feeding the five thousand shows us that God can do so much with so little! With only five loaves of bread and two fish, he fed five thousand people! His power is unmeasurable if you will just have faith, implore him, and trust him!

As done with the numbers, colors also have representations. We can do the same kind of exploration into the bells, smells, and the other theatrics of the mass. While I call them *theatrics* what they are in many cases is small *t*—traditions that have been passed down from the time of Jesus to before. Something we learned through the lay formation program is along with the small traditions are big *T—Traditions* that are absolute. I'll leave this google search in your hands if you want to learn more of the traditions of the church.

Real quick on a few colors: Purple is symbolic of wealth, prosperity, and luxury. Red is symbolic to the blood of Jesus, love of God, blood of lamb, atonement, salvation. Green stands for ordinary times. Rose is for our blessed mother, and the colors go on.

When you go to mass, pay attention to everything that is going on around you. All the symbols, saints, colors, emblems, paintings, flowers, the layout of the church, everything has a story or deep-seeded meaning. Many stories come from the Bible. When we sit and ponder the church, it is good to dig deep into the stories (the bells and the smells) that tell the life and times of the church.

I hope this book has provided a little enlightenment into what John 3:16 means. My hope is that you take the small enlightenment and explore the inside world of Christianity: God, Jesus, the Holy Spirit. May you be blessed and always remember you are where you are for a reason. Bless others today with the truths that are given to us in the Bible. You are the only bible some people will ever hear. If you have been baptized, the priest blessed you "priest, prophet, king" (Catechism of the Catholic Church, 897–913). Put on that authority and share the Bible as God intended you to share. Remember we don't have to know everything. The Bible, its church and members are all around us to clarify God's love. The Bible, its church and members are all around us to clarify God's salvation intent (John 3:16.5).

Luke 15:3–7

Jesus addressed this parable to the Pharisees and scribes: "What man among you having a hundred sheep and losing one of them would not leave the ninety-nine in the desert and go after the lost one until he finds it? And when he does find it, he sets it on his shoulders with great joy and, upon his arrival home, he calls together his friends and neighbors and says to them, 'Rejoice with me because I have found my lost sheep.' I tell you, in just the same way there will be more joy in heaven over one sinner who repents than over ninety-nine righteous people who have no need of repentance."

Bridge the Gap

As I near the end of this book, I can't help but think, where would I suggest a person start reading the Bible? How can you start playing your role in *bridging the gap*? Hopefully you've already began, but if you haven't and you want more, one suggestion often made is begin with reading Luke and go on to Acts from there. Luke wrote both books, so it gives you a quick jump and continuum into the story of Jesus. From the end of Acts, some recommendations say go back to the beginning of the New Testament (Matthew) and read through the four Gospels. Pay attention to the footnotes that will refer you to the different Gospels for the same readings. Option 2 from Acts is just to continue reading forward into the New Testament books (Romans on out to the Revelation). Option 3 for me was I went back to the beginning of the Old Testament book of Genesis and set my mind to begin reading. Every day, I woke up fifteen to thirty minutes early before going to work, and I would read fifteen, twenty, thirty minutes a day. It took me over a year to complete the book, but once you get going, you're not going to want to stop. Everything will start to come together, *especially* after having read this book, *John 3:16.5*. The Bible is so rich with information and lessons and love. I hope this book has been a blessing to you. Bless someone else and pass it on. Never forget

1 Corinthians 12:20
"We are many parts, yet one body."

When you embrace that scripture statement, you are going to realize like a map at Disney World, "You are here." Here is exactly where God intended you to start. (Reference the appendix for a nice reflection on jumping *all in*.) Start with your family, neighbors, friends, the community, the church. God has placed you exactly where you are for your particular mission. You have all the tools you need; your friends and family are all around you. Begin doing God's called ministry and you're going to discover you are doing *God's will* or you're now walking God's intended purpose in life for you. One thing (job, year, season) will lead to another. Never stop learning, never stop worshiping. Always give God his thanks, and He's going to reward you back.

Closing Quiz

I thought it would be fun to test what you have learned. In the following Bible parable script, answer to yourself the following questions. Who represents Jeremiah? Who represents the Potter? Who is the clay? What is the Word of God? What is the Potter doing to the clay? Who is Israel?

Jeremiah 18:1-6 This word came to Jeremiah from the LORD: Rise up, be off to the potter's house; there I will give you my message. I went down to the potter's house and there he was, working at the wheel. Whenever the object of clay which he was making turned out badly in his hand, he tried again, making of the clay another object of whatever sort he pleased. Then the word of the Lord came to me: Can I not do to you, house of Israel, as this potter has done? says the LORD. Indeed, like clay in the hand of the potter, so are you in my hand, house of Israel.

Welcome to the Christian family! If you read this book up to here, I am confident you received the Word and interpreted the parable, according to God's will. Did you feel the chills, get the goosebumps? Did your throat lump up? Did something unusual happen? Did you cry or get emotional? God loves *you*! That's Jesus, God, the Holy Spirit screaming at you from within his temple (your body). Receive it and go forward!

With that, I'll finish with a "God's people" chant (it's like a code or secret true brother-sister handshake). And *all* of God's people said:

> ME. God is good!
> YOU. All the time!
> ME. All the time!
> YOU. God is good!

Go and preach the good news! Spread the love!

Call to action: I went to mass this morning. Upon the end of mass, the priest announced there will be no mass tomorrow due to the fact that we do not have enough priests. If you have a calling to serve the church—whether it's to be a priest, usher, lecture, deacon, nun, pastor, groundskeeper, prayer minister, eucharistic minister, meals minister, administrator, accountant, on and on—please reach out to your church and ask them where you can start, where you can help, whether there are any openings. Oh by the way, did you know the Catholic Church does accept some married pastors from other denominations? Inquire. You may fit right in. (Reference the appendix for a few articles on What's the Deal About Legally Married Priests? or If Today You Hear His Voice, Harden Not Your Heart. Not 100 percent sure where to start? Consider the church families' new journey through the world—National Eucharistic Revival.)

APPENDIX

Resources

Unites States Conference of Catholic Bishops (USCCB's) website (https://www.usccb.org/)

Unites States Conference of Catholic Bible (https://bible.usccb.org/bible)

The USCCB Approved Bible Translations (https://www.usccb.org/offices/new-american-bible/approved-translations-bible).

Catechism of the Catholic Church (https://www.usccb.org/sites/default/files/flipbooks/catechism/)

What exactly do most Christians profess to?

- Nicene Creed (https://www.usccb.org/beliefs-and-teachings/what-we-believe)
- Apostles' Creed (https://www.usccb.org/prayers/apostles-creed)

Guide to Confession—Adults guild to reconciliation (https://svdp-peoria.com/assets/uploads/documents/sacraments/adultconfessionguide.pdf)

"The Structure and Meaning of the Mass" (https://www.usccb.org/offices/public-affairs/structure-and-meaning-mass)

"What's the Deal About Legally Married Priests?" (https://www.ewtn.com/catholicism/library/whats-the-deal-about-legally-married-priests-1079)

Catholic Daily Reflections (https://catholic-daily-reflections.com)

"Fidelity in Suffering" (https://catholic-daily-reflections.com/2022/

08/28/fidelity-in-suffering/)
"Demons Are For Real" (https://catholic-daily-reflections.com/2022/
08/29/demons-are-for-real/)
"The Keys of the Kingdom" (https://catholic-daily-reflections.
com/2022/08/03/the-keys-of-the-kingdom/)
"All In!" (https://catholic-daily-reflections.com/2022/08/18/being-
all-in-2/)
"Attentiveness to Jesus" If today you hear his voice, harden not
your heart. (https://catholic-daily-reflections.com/2022/08/27/
attentiveness-to-jesus-2/)

Free Bibles

Bible Study. I have this Bible downloaded onto my phone. Priceless
in searches, and it also has the ESV and King James Version of
the Bible. My recommendation is to stick with the ESV as it is
meant for easy English reading and it's also the Bible version we
follow at church.
Gideon Bible App. Free for iOS and Android phones. Has 1,100 lan-
guages.
Hope House. I'm told Hope House offers Bibles.
MyFreeBible.org. Offers a hard copy, half a Bible. The New Testament
for free.

Free helpful apps

Evangelizo. This app gives you the daily readings, canticle, Gospel,
commentary, and more information such as Saint Days, etc.
Mass Times. Don't leave home without it. Anywhere you go around
the world, look for and find a church nearest you. It will give
you the Mass and reconciliation times. Priceless!
The Daily Motivator. Ralph Marston. Daily messages intended to
remind and bring you back, day after day, to the best that's
within you.

Shift (How can we shift from an old life to a new life?)

Christian radio. Tune into Christian radio in the lower FM frequencies. I like listening to K-Love (usually 88.1), a national Christian station where you can listen to modern contemporary music practically anywhere you go. In the same frequency range, you'll also find Catholic radio stations and some Christian talk shows as well. If you tune into iHeart radio, Joel Osteen has a good encouraging podcast. *Be advised and be alert*, there are some radical thinkers about what Christianity is. If it doesn't "feel" right, move on. Listen for the *love*, and you'll find the Christian heart.

Journey Home. Marcus Gordi, EWTN Network. This is my personal weekly favorite show on EWTN. I love to listen to the stories of all the denominations, their realization moments, and their insights. what they went through, what they felt and what they found (https://www.ewtn.com/tv/shows/journey-home).

Daniel Adami. On Spotify (https://open.spotify.com/artist/585Z-RVGBgh6LQfFf6o5NQP).

What can you jump into that would be invigorating for your journey?

National Eucharistic Revival. If you live in the United States, the Catholic church just announced a new National Eucharistic Revival movement to launch in 2023. This appears like it will be a perfect on ramp back into the church or God's intended fullness (https://www.eucharisticrevival.org/learn-resources).

ACTS. ACTS is a three-day retreat usually held at a site away from the local parish. It was named for the four topics covered: adoration, community, theology, and service.

The Encounters (Others). Brother Gerardo Hernandez, founder of Body of Christ (BOC) Ministry, authored and brought to our parish "The Encounters." This was my first retreat experience (five weeks of a couple hours study, a retreat, then five more weeks of study—invaluable). As I told my friends, family, others, when you go to a retreat it's like going to an "underground" community (in a really good way). Here is where we find the laity on fire for the Lord. Assuring to everyone through the process was Gerardo, along with their trained and prepared table leaders, the priests, nuns, plus a host of other team members that supported the event.

Cursillo. One of the older movements of the church, which has withstood a test in time, has been the Cursillo. Like the prison ministry movement, the apostolate of the laity has its purpose in the Christianization of the world through apostolic action of Christian leaders. A three-day period of spiritual renewal stressing the dynamic, communitarian, and personalistic aspects of the Christian faith.

Rite of Christian Initiation of Adults (RCIA). This program outlines the steps for the formation of catechumens, bringing their conversion to the faith to a greater maturity. It also helps them respond more deeply to God's gracious initiative in their lives and prepares them for union with the church community.

Lay Formation. It is an academic and pastoral formation program for Catholic men and women interested in taking the *next step* on their Christian journey. Lay Formation is about forming people by learning more about our faith, our belonging to a vibrant Catholic community, deepening our relationship with God, and increasing our prayer life. Cora and I went through the three-year program. We received our three medals per year, and in the end, we received our diploma for religious instructions. We mounted the medals and diploma in a shadow box that hangs in our sitting room. In our house you will not find our degrees or certificates or anything else on the walls, but we were particularly proud or pleased to complete this course in its entirety. It was truly enlightening into the full understanding of the Catholic Church. A full three-year study of the catechism of the Catholic Church.

If your churches do not have a choice of the suggested above and beyond activities, encourage your church or diocese to reach out, get help, start. I know Brother G traveled the country, helping churches igniting fire, the Holy Spirit, within themselves.

A NOTE TO THE RECIPIENT OF THIS BOOK

Beloved (as God would have addressed you),

You are all God intended you to be. Like a puzzle piece of life, you are critical to his unimaginable reveal. While you have been gifted your unique perspectives and views in life, so have everyone else around us been given their unique perspectives and views. In a world of eight billion people, humans are ever-evolving.

Sometimes you may be in a place where another unique piece is mentoring you. Sometimes you will be mentoring others. Every step you take, every place you go, you are either learning, teaching, or maybe you are just filling in a gap.

Know you have the tools where you are. Allow God's timing to work for you as he is working his timing for everyone else around us. While you may not be in your designated role today, know your lead or purpose role is coming. Continue growing, open yourself to God's forming words. Never give up early, thinking something was not meant to be.

Relax, enjoy life, smell the roses. Trust you are learning and doing things of unimaginable value for your future. God's timing and ways are different from ours. Like mysteries, understanding comes with time. Allow God to build you up to the person he has intended you to be. Rome was not built in a day. God's plan, with his only beloved son, took thirty-three years, plus, to come to full fruition.

Let go, let God. Trust, he has enormous things in store for you and everyone who welcomes him into their life.

May God bless you and give you peace!

Wally G!

CHARITY/PHILANTHROPY

Proverbs 11:25
Be generous, and you shall be prosperous.
Help others, and you shall be helped.

As a lifelong believer and fairly-early contributor to various charities, I commit at least thirty percent of all profits from this book to not only to the church but to other warriors for Christ.

- Catholic charities
- Men and women formations and prison ministries
- Men, women, children's shelters
- The American Red Cross,
- The Salvation Army
- American Cancer Society
- Driscoll Children's Hospitals
- Food banks
- Hope House
- Others

Never judge or, better said, judge wisely your gifts. Always give from the heart, and always give with good intentions. What I have learned through my contributions in life is God really loves a giving heart. You will never out-give God.

Feel the spirit of giving. Commit to volunteer at one or several of the volunteer sites or, another good deeds organization of your choice. The ministries are unlimited, fulfilling, and rewarding beyond words.

May God bless you, and thank you for supporting the cause!

ABOUT THE AUTHOR

Wally Gonzalez Jr. is a born and raised Christian Catholic. Rich in Spanish Tejano culture; religion was not something he perceived as the "mans" duty. As he matured, he began to listen to evangelical and apostolic ministries. His heightened interest into the healing and other ministries began to reveal themselves through the exponential expansion of cable television. He would hear and read about the powers of the Holy Spirit through the Word, but he was naively unaware of the Holy Spirit's presence. He began to question if it even existed in the Catholic church.

In the nineties, he was captivated by the popular fictional book series of Left Behind (Tim LaHaye and Jerry B. Jenkins). The series quickly lost his interest as he realized what he was reading was just not real. From that dabble, he ventured into more serious Christian studies and interests. A major turning point came when they moved back to Texas.

A thriving Catholic Church was a new experience to him. As he was adjusting into the modern, contemporary church, he began to be distracted again. One day he challenged himself, or better yet, he challenged his wife (as he still perceived the woman to be the lead to religion in the house) to attend a program (Alpha, which went on to mature into "The Encounters.)" For once, as the man of the house, he went above and beyond what he had ever done.

Today, Wally professes himself as a proud Catholic. While his faith, belief, understanding, and love for God have increased dramatically, he feels his humor, love for sports, and life have remained fulfilled. Asked for an explanation, he expanded, "I think I perceived the life of a religious person to be one of seclusion or exclusion." To my surprise, my life expanded into a life of fellowship with hundreds-upon-hundreds of brothers and sisters. Christians play ball, work out, shoot pool, go to movies, etc. We show up when we have a loss or when someone is in need. It is good to have found such a large supportive family of believers living and building each other up in God's salvation and grander plan.